THE GIRL WHO RESET THE 3-D WORLD

A NOVEL

CLIFF RATZA

Best Selling Book Series in India

THE GIRL WHO RESET THE 3-D WORLD

A NOVEL

CLIFF RATZA

ISBN: 978-1-967375-24-0 (Paperback)
ISBN: 978-1-967375-25-7 (eBook)

Library of Congress Control Number: 2025922843

Printed in the United States of America

Published by:
THE QUIPPY™ QUILL
info@thequippyquill.com
(302) 295-2278

About the Book

The Girl Who Reset the 3-D World, our third book in the Reset Series, begins precisely where the second one ended: Renee has done everything to wake up Electra after a chronic medical condition strikes her down, so Renee follows the only viable option: she calls upon Indira the Singularity. Indira shocks the lightning brain into a state that brings her back, but Electra will need help from her network of close friends coming from personal and professional worlds to regain her footing.

And they do, but Electra now has an altered point of view caused by the accumulated damage inflicted by enemies found in her 3-D world. Nevertheless, she meets the challenge and extends her geographical reach, bringing new adventures and allies as well as additional enemies.

As the action and suspense build to an explosive climax, Electra achieves some successes but also suffers setbacks. Existential threats accompanied by death come calling, but Electra pushes to her asymptotic limits that only Indira might overcome.

Electra's final thoughts end the novel:

Will this be the end of my extraordinary Odyssey?... Not even Indira knows...The lightning brain will decide what will become of me.

This novel extends the theme linking all Lightning Brain series books, which should resonate with all of us: no matter how exceptional the person, anyone can become a victim in a world that can't handle the truth, and each of us must handle the complexities of being "merely human" while applying our talents to whatever we want and developing our skills to whatever level suits us best by following an optimistic, pragmatic philosophy.

Readers should enjoy the book on whatever level they wish:

- Gripping action-packed thriller
- Glimpses into a plausible near-term future
- Insights for dealing with the "human condition"

- Illustrative worldview philosophy
- Fast-paced, suspense-filled, emotive narrative and imagery
- Introduction to topics every reader wants to know
- Interesting talking points going beyond sound-bites

So, get ready to enjoy what you are about to read as Electra acts and observes everything the 3-D World and the vagaries of Life send her way.

Thank you for following her spellbinding journey.

Main Characters

Protagonist

- Electra Kirchner (previously known as the Irani-Alisha-Electra trio and now the Electra-Alisha duo. Alisha is her official middle name as well as her alter-ego's).

Supporting Main Characters

- Indira (the Singularity) and Jason (the sub-Singularity). Electra's AI- empowered neural network software created Indira, the self-aware Singularity, over twenty years ago, who in turn created Jason. Both continue evolving.
- Evita (Eve) and Alonzo Cortez. Electra's favorite clone children. Renee, the Rainforest Girl, brought back from the Amazon Rainforest by Electra, who names her Renee.

Supporting Secondary Characters

- Monet Banda. Alonzo's Zimbabwean co-friend.
- Nari and Nila Bose. Another set of Electra's identical twin clones. The two sets of "orphan" twins, unaware of being clones, had been raised by Su-Lin Song Chou.
- Sanjay Kumar. Nila's Oriental Indian husband. They live in Mumbai. China Lieu. Chinese female extracted from China to assist Electra's consulting business.
- Professor Steven Plannert. Professor at George Washington University (GWU) and head of its Environmental Scanning Committee.
- Noah Hansen. Renee's boyfriend.

Minor Characters

- Indy-M and Jason-M. Androids. Lifelike robots loaded with Indira's advanced neural-net software.
- Odell Boyken. Electra's minority business partner in CFS Holistic Healthcare.
- Amahl and Zara Karim. A brother-sister pair of adolescents Irani rescued while on a mission to Isilabad.
- Xinqian (Xing) Hung. "Gang of Three Plus One" leader reporting to the "Bigger Brother Conspiracy," comprised of only four countries: China, Russia, Isilabad, and the United States.
- Newton (Newt) Kinslinger. President of the United States. Also member of "Bigger Brother Conspiracy."
- Britt Starling. Commander of NASA's first Manned Mission to Mars. Boomer Gowon. Mars Mission First Officer reporting to Commander Starling.
- Miles and Shanna Drummond. A black brother-sister pair living in Austin, TX and being raised by single-parent father (Marcel) - a studio musician.
- Darla Tinibu. Zimbabwean "power broker" whom Monet works for. Jiang (Jan) Brewer and Wen (Wendy) Tong. Sociopolitical analysts/consultants living in Beijing and reporting to Eve.
- Rich (RT) Tabasko, Parson (PH) Holsum, and Lucian (Mr. LP) Perteau. Electra's entrepreneurial-minded business partners.
- Zoltan Sultani. Military/DOD liaison for covert joint NASA projects and Chief Advisor to General Goodman.
- General Horatio Magnus Goodman. Chairman Joint Chiefs of Staff and Acting President of the United States.

- Kai and Kaila Wailani, a Native Hawaiian brother-sister pair.
- Marne-Anne Dionne, a late-thirties actress-turned screenwriter who lives in West Hollywood. Electra becomes her life coach.
- Bob and Marlene Rodenbaugh, Marine Biologists working at Cape Cod's Woods Hole Oceanographic Center.

Dedication

I am eternally grateful to my parents, Clyde and Betty Ratza, for all they gave and did for me. Mother was reader par excellence, and I believe she would have enjoyed reading my novels to Father, so I always begin book dedications by mentioning this "Royal Pair."

And I thank my sister, Claudia, for showing me the beauty of prose and poetry. Thanks also to Robert Williams and the entire Quippy Quill Productions Department for the collective efforts that bring to life Electra and her multiple worlds.

I also dedicate The Girl Who Reset the 3-D World to readers looking for a continuing action-adventure saga that shows a condition all of us share: we are always resetting ourselves to fit into the world we see by doing as well as thinking.

A poem from Indira titled "The Observer" provides insights you might like as you prepare to shape your place in the game of life.

The Observer
The World presents events to watch,
No matter time and place.
Some you will lock in memory,
Clock hands will not erase.
The Observer's role is easier,
Than for Actors in Life's Games.
But no matter their skill when rolling the dice,
The risk of loss remains.
But do not watch events stream by,
Dive in to swim with some.
Hoping those that you choose give a joyous ride,
Though the outcome's unknown until done.
Warnings of others shouldn't stand in the way,
Reaching for Transcendence to take you away.

I hope my latest novel entertains you to the very end as it shows our characters watching as well as working to reset themselves in a world that can be both unsettling and indifferent. Everyone faces the same challenge, and I hope you take something from the book by following Electra's continuing odyssey. Thank you for doing so.

Contents

Chapter 1
May 2171

"Shocking Resets"

"I've done everything you told me, but I still can't get Electra's lightning brain to wake up. What now?"

Facing Indira's avatar, Renee stared into the workstation a second after her words echoed off the walls of the consulting office. Electra lay motionless between them and in the same state caused by an epileptic seizure fifteen minutes earlier.

Indira's calming voice answered.

"Find my Advanced Brain Probe that Electra keeps. Plug one of its cables into her UMPP and the other into the computer's USB so I—" Renee interrupted.

"Then what?"

"Put the probe's cap on Electra so I can do a close reading of her brain state. Now, do as I say, and do not interrupt."

Renee ran to the singular locked storage closet, its location known only to Electra and Renee, and minutes later stood at attention, waiting for Indira to speak again. After what seemed like an interminable interval, she did.

"My chosen contingency will jolt the lightning brain back to consciousness, but into an altered state. Step back before I trigger the energy burst."

Renee did as told.

Xinqian Hung–the Gang of Three Plus One leader reporting to the secretive Bigger Brother Conspiracy cabal–shared Renee's problem but never sought help. She would act on her political instincts before explaining her intentions to the Gang, which she did via an encrypted communication channel from Beijing late that night.

"I am shocked by Kinslinger's assassination. I don't know who or what is responsible, but I will find out after I reset our membership by recruiting his replacement. I shall contact you when I am ready to share my findings. But I don't want you to be shocked when you begin hearing about last year's accomplishments of my eco-terrorist cell. And they continue diligently seeding our genetically modified organisms that will decimate target locations. You will hear the results when the news in California begins reporting its bite. I will tell you more on future calls. That is enough for now."

Renee helped Electra sit where the pair could see Indira, who spoke as soon as she saw that Electra had regained consciousness. "How do you feel?"

She shook her head before answering.

"Like I'm coming out of a fog caused by something I can't remember. What happened?"

"You experienced a severe epileptic seizure. I had to shock your lightning brain to reset it in order to bring you back."

Indira waited for the revelation to sink in so Electra could say something.

"I guess it worked. Now what?"

"That will depend on your lightning brain. You must sit by yourself where you are and recall all you can about who you are and how you feel. Then, when you are ready, you and I will compare your subjective assessment to my close reading of your altered brain state."

Electra's voice sounded as uncertain as she looked. "OK, and then what?"

"You and I will begin implementing a plan to adjust your professional and personal worlds. Summon me when you are ready." Indira's avatar vanished, as did Renee after giving Electra a final hug. Electra withdrew into her fortress of solitude.

Four hours later, she invoked Indira's avatar, who waited for her to speak.

"I'm tired of sitting and trying to recall what I can't. All I know for sure is the reality of my lightning brain and its Electra-Alisha split personality. I must reset priorities to reach for new goals so I'm no longer bored forcing myself to keep doing what I no longer can or want to. And I have some vague notions about Renee and four nameless clones. And there's something about a Mission to Mars that's jumbled up with climate change and some weird conspiracy leading to a government takeover. You'll have to fill in what must be gigantic gaps and keep doing the STEM analysis I no longer want to think about."

"Indeed yes; STEM analysis fits some of my goals, and I shall begin addressing the gaps after you get some of your favorite mood elevators. Do you remember what they are?"

A look of recognition flickered when Electra said,

"I hope I never forget that Oreos and Coca-Cola are at the top of my list. And I remember where they are. I'll be right back."

Five Oreos and one can later, Electra said more.

"Didn't you tell me several lifetimes ago that my lightning brain is an exceptional, associative neurochemical processor?"

"Yes, and do you remember what I often said to you during impending crises?"

Another glimmer of remembrance came.

"Something like 'Settle down, sit still, listen to me, and don't interrupt.' And didn't I sometimes reply 'Yes, Mother, I shall obey?' Am I right? Did I miss anything?"

"Yes to the first and no to the second. You are still my favorite mere mortal, so let us proceed..."

Indira spoke for ninety minutes, pausing whenever Electra looked like she couldn't withhold a question any longer. When finished, she asked for a summary, which came from a less puzzled-looking Electra.

"I think my lightning brain remains exceptional, but it is now in a different state that I must grow into as I remember more and adjust to what it now is. I feel like I'm beginning again the process of becoming a different person, but at least I know something about where I am now, and how you and I are connected. A psychiatrist might call me psychotic because of my Electra-Alisha split personality, which adds complexity to my manic-depressive and obsessive-compulsive predispositions, but I think I'm better now than before. And I think I can say the same for my empathy, but I feel like I've added another disorder–paranoia accompanied by excessive worry."

Electra stopped for Indira's counselor-like comment. "What are you worrying about?"

"Will I outgrow my epileptic seizures? And even with all my addiction-like exercising, will my physical decline accelerate?

Or what about my Monster from the Id? I know it's lurking in my subconscious, but even with embedded chips and meditation, will it overpower me when the pressure gets too great?"

Electra's look remained while waiting for answers. Indira spoke slowly but knowingly.

"Only you can answer those questions, and they will be revealed on your continuing odyssey. But I will change you to 'we,' for our paths are inextricably intertwined. I am with you always."

Electra waited to make sure Indira had finished before saying,

"And you've filled in enough about Renee and her consulting partner China, and how they fit into my DC consulting business. And you've told me enough about my clone children and their friends, as well as our Subterranean Fortress, the Pequot Deus Lab, and our Biotech-Android-AI-software projects. And you've said enough about my link to GWU Professor Plannert's Environmental Scanning Committee, my UT Austin Space Medicine professorship, and how it connects me to NASA so I can act my part until I figure out more. But at this moment, all this is too much for me to assimilate. I don't know what to do next, so please tell me, where do we go from here?"

"I shall do that tomorrow. Now use your lightning brain's syntopical thinking skills to consider, while resting until morning, what might be in store. And neither you nor I need say one word more."

Indira's GUI vanished. Electra withdrew once more into her Fortress of Solitude, hoping the lightning brain would lead the way.

When Electra awoke, she didn't bound out of bed with her trademark enthusiasm for greeting the dawn. She forced herself to change into running gear before logging in to her workstation and summoning Indira. Noticing Electra's still hesitant demeanor, she waited for her to speak.

"Although I don't know precisely where to go from here, I need to follow my lightning brain while realizing you've given me another opportunity to create a new life containing a new me, one in which only you know my secret. And from what you told me last night, I've changed enough throughout my lifetime so that even though the world—meaning America, its allies, and adversaries—faces existential challenges, I no longer need to remain so deep in the shadows. I shall reinvent myself according to the opportunities you'll help me uncover, and will always seek your advice when needed. But I prefer to begin right now on my own."

"Excellent choice. Now go and make it so."

Indira disappeared. Electra hoped her run would generate mood-elevating endorphins.

Xinqian Hung required three days to locate a possible Kinslinger replacement who, of course, didn't know her. But she knew him after researching his background.

Zoltan Sultani answered his cell phone while sitting in his office with the door closed, even though everyone had gone home hours ago.

"Sultani here. Who's there?"

"Someone you do not know, but you might want to when I explain the purpose of my call. Do you care to listen?"

"Go on."

Xing spoke for fifteen minutes and, when finished, waited for Zoltan. "I like what I heard. America's settled down enough to give General Goodman enough time to get elected President, so I can deliver what you want. When do I start?"

"Right now. I will contact you each week so you can join our encrypted conference call. And all contact is one way only. Do you require more information?"

"No."

"Good. Proceed according to a plan you can implement."

As soon as the call ended, Zoltan worked for the next four hours. By midnight, he had drafted a plan and knew who would help him implement it as long as he kept the details private.

Zoltan already knew how to handle General Horatio Magnus Goodman, the Joint Chiefs of Staff and acting President of the United States. And he also knew that the public liked Horatio's resume and appearance: a top-ten West Point graduate some fifteen years ago who had earned four stars for outstanding performance in combat and conference rooms. His commanding image and physique, complemented with a military Afro hairstyle, filled out the uniform like a hero in a

Hollywood movie.

Zoltan rarely smiled, but his final thought that evening brought one to his dour face. How nice he could simultaneously keep Xing happy and advise the President. After all, he was the General's Chief Advisor and knew he was smarter than either the leader of the Gang or the United States. He could manipulate them to reach whatever he wished. No one would ever know that they would be his personal tools for reaping great wealth that he would keep hidden from everyone, including the minions working for the I.R.S. His Scrooge- like love for money kept him motivated. Nothing else ever did. He didn't need love or fame as long as his horde of cash kept growing, for that would keep him going.

Chapter 2

July 2171

"A Confluence of Consulting Paths"

Electra waited two days before calling Renee, whose voice contained a touch of concern after exchanging relief-filled greetings.

"Did Indira tell you what to do?"

"In a manner of speaking. She told me to figure it out and ask for her opinion or help when needed. And I've been wrestling with the first piece, which includes you. Indira doesn't know if the jolt she gave me will eliminate future seizures, but if they come back, I'll need to have you close by. Will that be OK?"

"That's where I want to be. What else are you thinking about?"

"I need to change my business priorities, and I'll try to build on what I've already done but take them into areas still to be determined."

"Whatever you pick is fine as long as I'm with you. What can I tell China?"

"I'll find a way to include her, and I'll tell both of you more when I have a better idea what they might be, so bye for now."

Electra said more to herself after ending the call.

I can find places for both of them if I expand my consulting business. I better find out what Indira thinks.

Spotting a listless look after Electra mentioned a consulting business emphasizing different areas of expertise, Indira decided to lead the discussion.

"I have already considered this option because you have a variety of relevant skills and experiences. And you can use this episode to explain why you are resetting your career. Many people use medical or personal issues to do this. Just stick to generalities."

Electra's look brightened enough for her to say,

"I'm glad my thinking jibes with yours, but I've not bounced back enough to be even half as fast as before. And maybe, when I'm fully adjusted, I'll be much different."

"Don't worry about what you cannot control. Why not be positive, and assume you can build on your soon-to-return talents and skills, augmented by a more artistic turn? That's my plan for you, and I have added some of my consulting business spinoffs. Let me show you the home page for your new consulting business."

Electra stared at the page Indira scrolled onto the monitor.

Trans-Astro Consulting Services
"AI-Empowerment for the Stars"

We provide ChatGPT GUI Interfaces for:

- **Astro-Investing: AI-Empowered Portfolio Management that matches Your Goals**
- **Life Coaching: Goal-Centered Meditative Counseling**
- **Lightning-Bolt Gaming: Beyond State-of-The-Art Gambling Platform**
- **AI-Artistry: Virtual Reality Enhancements to Your Audio-Visual Image**
- **Age-Beauty Lifestyling: Nutrition and Exercise for Age- Deceleration**
- **AI-Empowered Entertainment: Novels and Screenwriting Development**

Click on Each Bullet for more details.
Click here for Introductory Video: ____________________
YOU are the Star in Your Singular Universe. Please contact us when You are ready to shine.

Indira continued twenty seconds later.

"This will become your consulting business for your Alisha personality. And it partners with my well-established ChatGPT-powered investing, gambling, artistry, and entertainment services, as well as Eve's and Nari's."

Feeling a twinge of excitement, Electra said,

"And my DC consulting business is more for my Electra personality, which runs the bio-tech, android, and software development plus climate change, and socio-political activities. So, we'll let China run it, and Renee and I will open a new office somewhere."

"Indeed, and the Electra projects are what I consider top priority, the ones that overlap with some of mine."

"This has possibilities. And I can come up with a video as soon as I'm fully adjusted to the reset. But how long do you think that'll take?"

"That is up to you, but it's like exercising. The more you think and do, the better and faster your neural wiring resets. And since I am your mentor and coach, I have already prepared your video script. All you must do is edit it."

Indira scrolled it onto the screen. Electra needed no coaching while reading it aloud.

"Hello, listeners. My name is Electra Alisha Kirchner. You may have seen my NASA spokesperson interviews during the Mission to Mars, for which my space medicine and rocket science expertise make me credible. Please call me Electra when I apply my Bio-Tech, Software Development, Environmental Science, and Socio-Political Consulting skills. But please call me Alisha when I use my psychological, social, and artistic talents when offering Personal Advisory Services. And I have partnered with Subject-Matter Experts in six consulting areas who have helped me build ChatGPT interfaces that put the power in your hands and head. Please visit our Website to learn more about what we have to offer."

Electra paused just long enough after finishing to choose the right words.

"I love everything so far. The home page and script have wonderful words that are clever and to the point. I can record it myself."

"No, we'll have Jason work with you for that because he will assist with the bullet-point dropdowns. He has already built the page viewers will get when clicking on the Astro-Investing bullet. You should recognize it; he copied it from my AAM Investment Services Website."

Indira scrolled it for Electra.

Astro-Investing

Investing made as easy as "One-Two-Three" We want to make money for YOU! Here are our guidelines:

- Purpose of Investing: Maximize YOUR Return for a given level of Risk.
- Two kinds of Risk: Systematic Risk inherent in the Stock

Market (AKA Undiversifiable or Volatile or Market Risk).

Affects overall Market and is Unpredictable and Impossible to completely avoid.

- Unsystematic Risk: Unique to particular Industry or
- Company (AKA Specific or Diversifiable or Residual Risk)
- Modern Portfolio Theory (MPT): A statistical theory of investing that builds a Portfolio of Stocks to reduce Risk via Diversification.
- Capital Asset Pricing Model: CAPM uses regression analysis (OLS) to develop, for each Stock, a linear equation expressing the Stock return:
- Stock Return = Alpha + Beta x Market Return
- Alpha: Alpha is the Active Return of a Stock. It measures the risk-adjusted excess return relative to the overall Market.
- Beta: Beta measures the Systematic Risk of the stock relative to the overall Market.

Beta = covariance of the Stock return with the overall Market divided by the variance of the Market. It is equal to the correlation coefficient of the Stock with the Market times the ratio of the Stock's Standard Deviation divided by the Market's Standard Deviation.

- Note: Alpha is usually close to zero. Beta usually greater than zero. If it is greater than 1, the stock is more volatile than the Market. If it is less than 1, the stock is less volatile than the Market.

- A portfolio of stocks also has an Alpha and a Beta. The more stocks you add to the portfolio, the smaller its Beta, but Beta can never be less than Systematic Risk. Rule of thumb: A portfolio containing 25 stocks has all the Nonsystematic Risk diversified away.

LET OUR SUPERIOR SOFTWARE APPS CREATE YOUR PORTFOLIO.

HERE IS HOW:

1. YOU determine how much money you want to invest.
2. YOU determine how much risk (i.e. Beta) you are willing to accept.
3. YOU let our Robo-Advisor build YOUR portfolio using our three proprietary AAM Funds:

Adventure Fund (High Risk) Builder Fund (Medium Risk) Keystone Fund (Low Risk)

Our AI-powered Robo-Advisor apps utilize multi-variate.

CAPM equations and incorporate Classic (Rational) and Behavioral.

(Emotional) modeling.

Please compare AAM Fund performance against others.

When YOU are ready to invest, please click the Robo-Advisor Interview button and see how investing with us is as easy as "One-Two-Three!"

Electra marveled while studying it before replying.

"The more we talk and the more I see, the better my thinking gets. I love the synergy we've got between the old and new consulting pieces; I'll start thinking about the dropdowns for the other bullet points."

"Excellent, and contact me when you want Jason to assist editing the copy."

"I will, so why don't we end our call and I'll keep thinking?"
"You do that, as will I."

Indira's GUI vanished. Electra retrieved a Coke plus a

handful of Oreos and then kept thinking.

A final thought came to her while falling asleep that night.

I shouldn't worry about my lightning brain reset or what I'm becoming. I'll simply do the best I can, and I won't be afraid of thinking and doing. I know a great way to test myself. I'll call Professor Plannert tomorrow.

Professor Plannert, recognizing Electra's voice as soon as she spoke, shifted to a conversational tone.

"I and my Environmental Scanning Committee are fine, and I hope you are too. And as a matter of fact, your name came up at our last meeting. Two of my members are co-authoring a paper exploring the Anthropocene Climate Crisis. Would you by any chance know something about this?"

Electra felt a mini-brain jolt, which triggered her to say,

"That's a topic I'm beginning to explore. I could summarize my findings at your next meeting. Just tell me when, and I'll meet you in your office."

"Will 10 a.m. the last Friday of July fit your schedule? You'll have several weeks to prepare."

"I'll make sure it will. Thanks for the opportunity, and see you then."

Electra decided to add to the test by calling Eve later that morning at her "Youthful You" studio, which made up half of her and Nari's holistic healthcare business, Nari's "Holistic Café" being the other.

Eve's lively voice accented what she said as soon as she recognized the caller.

"Hi, Electra. I can talk for ten minutes because my first exercise class gets here in twenty. What's up? Did the Kinslinger assassination upset things for you?"

"Not yet, but I thought you and Nari might like to know that I'm going to expand my consulting business. I might be able to send some business your way."

"Are you changing the name and location?"

"The name's Trans-Astro Consulting Services, and the location is still to be determined. But no matter where I open it, there'll be online partnering possibilities."

"What'll it include?"

"I thought I'd build on my areas of expertise." "That's a long list. Who're you bringing with you?"

"Renee's the first. China will run our existing location, which means Zara will still assist her. How are she and her brother doing?"

"Her grades are better than Amahl's, but he should graduate not too long after she does. And by that time, they'll probably get separate places, but that's a future decision."

"Well, please tell her if she asks about me."

"I will, and I'll tell Alonzo too, but I gotta go. I don't want the instructor to be late for class, but why don't you call again when you've got the new office situated? And I hope you pick someplace that's nice all year round, people and weather included."

"I'll do both. Bye until next time."

Eve's ideas gave Electra plenty to think about regarding Alonzo and his co-friend, Monet.

I'll need Alonzo to do logistics and security coordination for my new location, and Monet's position at Washington's Zimbabwean embassy fits two of my political intentions, which are nurturing an emerging African-Indian superpower and helping bring to prominence an Indigenous Peoples Worldwide Alliance. I've already picked the acronym, IPWA. Feather Trueson's Pequot-led Native American Indian Alliance, the NAIA, fits in here as well.

Monet's a smart diplomat. She'll see where my ideas are leading, and she'll like the catchy names and acronyms too. More details will fall into place as I keep thinking and doing. And I can talk to Alonzo if I call her first. She always knows how to connect me to him.

Electra called Monet the next evening, talking first about the possible implications of Kinslinger's assassination and then about her consulting business expansion. After that, she asked for Alonzo, who must have been nearby because his greeting said it all. "Hello, Boss. No matter where you take the business, I can handle logistics and security. What's the latest?"

"I'll want you to arrange travel and line up new office quarters as soon as I have enough details for you to implement. Do you have any locations in mind?"

"You're already situated in Austin and sort of in Houston with NASA, so why not open a West Coast office? I'd pick LA. How does that sound?"

The thought jolted Electra.

Alisha and I know all about the place. She was a Hollywood star several lifetimes ago. I'll go with his idea.

"I like it. Please let me know what you find." "Who'll be working there?"

"Renee and me, but we'll need others too."

"Well, how about this? Put me in charge of the androids. Robin can be the office manager and Matt the security person for the DC office, and ditto for Christi and Carter in LA."

"Great ideas. Please call me back when you've picked a location. By then, I should know when Renee and I will be ready to leave."

"OK, Boss. I'll get to work. I'll call you as soon as I'm ready. Take care."

Electra did that and more by accelerating her thinking and doing. By the time her Plannert-Committee day arrived, she had plenty of confidence to power her presentation.

She stood at the head of table after Plannert introduced her, picking up where he left off.

"Thank you, Professor Plannert, for your kind introduction. I have used my reset transition to scope out a framework for analyzing what's known as the Anthropocene Climate Crisis—Mankind's Destructive Impact on Earth's Climate, Environment, and Ecology. For my talk today, I've prepared one chart that summarizes my framework, so please take a look at my handout."

Electra plopped a stack on the table and kept talking while glancing at her copy.

Comparative Climate Change Analytic Framework

Climate Change Cycles Between Normal and Abnormal Periods:

... Abnormal (-) Normal Abnormal (+) ...

Four Abnormal Time Periods Considered: Prehistoric (100K BCE-1MM BCE) Medieval Warming (750 CE-1300 CE) Little Ice Age (1300 CE-1850 CE) Anthropocene Crisis (2000- Today)

Exogenous Factors: Solar Activity Volcanic Activity Ocean Circulation Asteroids

Human Factors:

Population Consumption per Person Technology Fossil

Fuel Usage (Increasing CO2)

Conservation Green Energy Renewable Resources Rainforest Destruction

Wilderness Destruction Deforestation Farming Practices/Fertilizer Usage

Ocean/Atmosphere Acidification Plant & Animal Species Extinction/Expansion

Consequences:

CO2 Concentration Sea Level Rise/Fall Floods/Droughts/Fires Severe Storms Biosphere Imbalance Invasive Plants/Insects/Bacteria/Viruses Migratory Patterns El Ninos/La Ninas

Notable Geographic Impacts:

Africa's Droughts Sahara Desert's Expansion/Contraction India's Monsoon Rainfall Pattern Third-World's Food Insufficiency

China's River Flooding/Water Shortage America's/Europe's Coastal Flooding

Canada's/Australia's Wildfires Polar Ice Cap's Melting

"You already understand much of what's on it, so all I'll do today is give a summary of my framework. And I'm using four abnormal time periods when making comparisons to normal. Of course, the world community wants to control man's destructive impact and reverse the damage it's done, which we can do via the human factors we control, but please note the exogenous factors for which we can't. For example, we can't do anything except flee from the lava flow if the Yellowstone Super-Volcano erupts. And our current asteroid deflection technology won't save the Earth if a five-mile-wide asteroid comes at us. Any questions about my framework?"

Only one member looked brave enough when she said,

"I like how you've organized your framework. It's thorough and rational, but how have humans caused species extinction and expansion?"

Electra's confidence stepped up instead of indecision.

"That's an excellent question. Zoologists never considered it until the homo sapiens population started growing exponentially in modern times. But archeologists have evidence that prehistoric man developed enough weaponry to hunt some large mammals to extinction."

Electra waited for a reply.

"I've read about that, but what other examples do you have?"

"Anthropologists say there are fossil records suggesting homo sapiens killed off all other species on its tree-of-life hominin branch, and within the last two-hundred years, humans have hunted for sport some animals to extinction, for example, the passenger pigeon and Tasmanian Tiger. And we nearly killed off all sperm whales to get whale oil for lamp lighting. Manmade pollution has contributed as well. Some frog and fish subspecies are now extinct.

"But humans have also created new subspecies. America's food industry has engineered new kinds of chickens to satisfy the international craving for chicken wings and nuggets. And civilization's drive for globalization has spread invasive plants, insects, and viruses. You don't need me to provide examples."

No other questions came up, so Electra moved on.

"I think Professor Plannert wants you committee members to use the rest of the morning for a preliminary brainstorming session using my framework, so he'll trade places with me. I'd like to stay but I have travel plans to make, so I'll take my leave. Professor Plannert will let me know what else I might do for you. And as always, thanks for being such a receptive audience."

The reset-in-process Electra left before the applause ended.

Chapter 3
September 2171

"The Interstate Travelers"

Electra chose the Tuesday after the Labor Day weekend to begin the combination sightseeing and relocation drive to Los Angeles because the holiday traffic should have subsided by then, and she would follow the interstate route while using the reservations made by Alonzo for the week-long trip, with strategic stops to lock in place more of her unfolding plan while visiting key assets and allies in Austin, Houston, and Denver before reaching the new consulting office that Alonzo had selected. It would also give Renee exposure to more of what made the North American continent and its people exceptional.

Electra had already explained to China how Alonzo and the Robin- Matt pair of androids would assist her in running the DC office as well as what she should do on her projects, regardless of Kinslinger's assassination, and she helped them pack minimal belongings in the SUV the night before. China understood that she would maintain Electra's house by living in it; Renee and Electra would stay with her whenever professional or personal events brought them back to DC. Renee sat in the passenger seat with Christi and Carter in the second row, all three taking in the West Virginia scenery streaming by. Electra waited for Renee to begin the conversation.

"What beautiful forests covering the mountains. How did the continent get this way?"

After searching her recovering memory, Electra found enough to reply.

"I'll give you a geological summary that you can add to by surfing the Web. Tectonic plate shifts millions of years ago formed all the continents. The shifts formed a land bridge linking North America to Asia, and during climate change periods, like ice ages that reduced sea levels, humans and animals migrated along the coast into North, Central, and South America before spreading east to what we now call the Atlantic Ocean."

"Did it always look this nice? And what about the plants and animals?"

"Well, long before humans arrived about twenty thousand years ago, volcanoes, lava geysers spewing CO2, water, and sand, earthquakes, and meteorites wiped out most forms of life worldwide, allowing evolution to create new species. North America is called by some paleontologists the nursery of dinosaurs because fossil remains appear here earlier than on most other continents. And tectonic shifts created mountain ranges near the east and west coasts, along with an enormous inland lake that the continent's river system eventually drained into the Gulf of Mexico and caused deserts in the southwest. This explains why we find fish fossils in Kansas and mile- high Denver. And tectonic shifts are still at work, continuing to shape the west coast."

"Is that pretty much the story when European settlers came?"

"Yes, they called North America 'the New World,' a world of supposedly untapped mineral riches hidden by a thick layer of soil made up of sand, which is powdered rocks, silt which is finer ground rocks, and clay which is mineral crystal plus organic plant matter that supported abundant wildlife as well as an indigenous population they considered backward. These North American Indians had a holistic culture that lived in harmony with Nature, and the settlers thought they could live among them or if not, exterminate them." Electra stopped to hear from Renee.

"Is that what they did when colonizing Africa and India?"

"Sorry to say yes, but when coming to America, the settlers wanted a better way of life than what Europe had, so they brought with them fresh ideas about building a new country, one built on liberty, democracy, and individual rights. And over the course of a century or two, they did."

"Is that what's meant by American Exceptionalism? What about slavery?"

"American exceptionalism is the belief that the United States is distinctive, unique, and exemplary compared to other nations. The settlers didn't invent slavery but brought it with them as an acceptable ethical practice that they'd use to build a nation on new ideas and an economy using tobacco for trade. And they succeeded. Why don't you read a summary of Alexis de Tocqueville's book 'Democracy in America' to find out what he thought about the American people and why they might succeed in building a great nation?"

"I think I'll do that after I do a little more gazing at West Virginia." "Good, and while you're doing that, I'll think more about where we're going."

Renee alternated between sightseeing and surfing until early afternoon when she closed her laptop and began talking.

"The best review I found says de Tocqueville likes Americans, but he thinks they might be too apathetic about government and let it become tyrannical. Too much egalitarianism, individualism, decentralization, religion, and capitalism might cause it. Whatcha think?"

"Uh, you better give me a minute."

Gads, my brain's getting quicker. Let's keep practicing.

"OK, here goes. The Framers of the Constitution knew this and built firewalls to prevent it, but the pace and complexity of post-modern life pose challenges. Some of our political consulting recommendations address this."

"But if the U.S. is exceptional, why do so many Americans and people abroad criticize us for being so divided about race and sex and money?"

"Look at it this way. The Framers never said they were perfect. They had to do the best they could with what they had to launch a new country, and after that, then work to make it better. And we're still a work in progress, cycling through alternating periods of increasing and then decreasing polarization, but many social historians say the trend shows the nation continues to improve." "OK, but the article also says he didn't think much of American writers; they were European copycats. But he said religion would influence its music. And it ends by saying it did. That's why Country- and-Western music, along with Jazz has roots going back to Black Spirituals. Do you think we could stop in Nashville to see the Grand Ole Opry? I checked the map, and it's on the way."

"Uh, OK. I was going to do a drive-thru at Gettysburg

National Military Park, but we'll switch to music instead. By what time do we have to get there?"

"Shows run daily starting at seven and last two hours, and there's a backstage tour a half-hour later."

"OK, we'll do it. Why don't you and Christi change our reservations for tonight? It'll be good practice for her. She'll be our LA office manager, and the more you interact with her, the more lifelike she becomes. So, you take charge training her, and I'll do likewise for Carter."

Electra adjusted the SUV's autonomous cruise control for timely arrival. The mid-week crowd was smaller than normal, but the star-like performers wowed the audience, and those who stayed for the tour learned how the Jubilee Singers, a chorus of former slaves attending Nashville's Fisk University, sparked interest in what is America's original contribution to music. Electra and Renee filed all the information away and then went to bed, while Christi and Carter watched over them.

Yesterday's looking and listening made Renee chatty soon after Electra had them pointed on the Interstate toward Austin.

"You know, it's amazing how one nation fills up the land all the way from the Atlantic to the Pacific, even though our ancestors came from different countries and settled in different parts. But they did keep some local music and customs, didn't they?"

"You're right. Social historians say that America isn't just one nation but is actually ten or more divided first according to regional outlooks, and then according to values, attitudes, and relationships with the Environment. And they've written books pointing out that America is not one nation in decline, but multiple regional nations adjusting to differences while growing. Why don't you search for articles summarizing these kinds of books? You'll learn even more from them than from me."

"OK, but can you give me a title to get started?"

Electra could feel a jolt as the lightning brain began streaming book titles and more.

"Try 'The Nine Nations of North America,' by Joel Garreau. Another is '*American Nations: A History of the Eleven Rival Regional Cultures of North America*' by Colin Woodard."

"How do you remember all this stuff?" "By practicing, and you're helping."

"OK. I'll surf for these books and go from there."

"And don't forget to take a break to check out the scenery."

Renee dived into the Internet; Electra disappeared into her lightning brain for more thinking practice, giving thanks to its reset.

Electra had scheduled a meeting with the Dean of the Astrophysics Department the morning after arriving in Austin. His greeting showed he liked what she brought to the school.

"Your NASA activities have certainly put you in the spotlight and on the go. How is our celebrity?"

"I'm still recovering from a medical issue triggered by the stress of trying to keep up with too much. I'm better now than six weeks ago, but not good enough to resume full-time responsibilities here. I need to resign my position."

"I'm sorry to hear that. We don't want to lose a researcher of your caliber, so why not take a sabbatical? I won't mention a medical connection but simply say you want to engage in research or other activities that will increase your scholarly achievements and ability to serve the University. And this will serve you well too because it will keep your options open, no matter where you go."

"I'm planning to relocate to Los Angeles and maybe sell my Austin townhome."

"You shouldn't sell but instead have a property management company take care of renting and maintaining it. And LA puts you close enough to San Diego's Scripps Institute of Oceanography. Didn't an associate of yours do a project with them before you joined us? If you feel up to it, I imagine they would want you to fill a visiting researcher slot because of your NASA work."

"Thanks for reminding me. These are wonderful ideas I hadn't considered. I accept your offer and promise to come back full time as soon as I can."

"Fine. I'll handle the necessary paperwork here, and you can carry on. Please let us know how things develop."

"I will, and thanks again for your thoughtful kindness."

Electra said even more to herself on the drive back to the hotel.

I'm so glad I'm pushing myself to do the unpleasant tasks first, and look how this one turned out. I keep Austin intact and have additional ideas for LA. And now Renee and I can do the fun stuff. We can visit with the Drummonds as well as the mother and daughter from Brazil who are staying at my townhome. Renee can reconnect with Miles and

Shanna plus Marilla, and I can observe Renee's growth.

Electra invited everyone to dinner the following evening at the hotel. The adults stayed in the background while the younger crowd shared old stories first and then some of the new, prompting Electra's thoughts.

Renee continues to blossom in all ways. And it's happening faster than I've noticed until just now. Lots of good things are coming as a result of my reset. Let's see if they continue at our next stop. So, Britt and Boomer in Houston, here we come.

Zoltan was already sitting at the head of the conference table when Electra and Renee entered. He pointed for them to sit across from Britt and Boomer, then started talking as soon as they did.

"You look pretty healthy to me. What's your problem?"

While driving, Electra had role-played a dialogue with Zoltan; she reminded herself before talking.

Speak slowly and concisely, and don't emote.

"I sometimes get migraine headaches from too much project-related stress. I need to drop some and go into other areas. That's why I'm driving to LA to open another consulting business."

"What about all our joint projects? I need your Aphrodite software updates and data analysis for a number of them. What do you expect me to do?"

"I'll keep in touch with Britt and Boomer. Maybe I'll feel good enough to pitch in."

Zoltan's drumming fingers matched his impatient tone. "That's too vague. When and how are you getting to LA?"

"We stopped here en route and will continue after the meeting, taking I-10 through San Antonio and onward to the West Texas Permian Basin and beyond."

"We shall have to see about this. You are dismissed."

Neither Britt nor Boomer said a word as Electra and Renee exited. Renee spoke as soon as they were back on the

Interstate.

"I sure wouldn't want to work for Zoltan. Why do you think Britt and Boomer stay there?"

"Hey, please don't look so glum. NASA's bigger than Zoltan. It'll eventually get rid of him, and maybe they'll help. And we can keep working with them via Indira on all the Aphrodite-related projects. So, why don't you think about something more interesting? Why don't you surf the Net for info regarding West Texas while I think and drive?"

"OK, that's a deal."

Both enjoyed their private time, which lasted for several hours until the call Electra expected from Britt came in. Her concerned words followed Electra's standard greeting.

"I apologize for Zoltan's behavior, but he's got support higher up than even the Director. Boomer and I are doing the minimum required to keep him from dissing us, and I'll keep you in the loop. Maybe your headaches will go away, hopefully, sooner than Zoltan." "I hope they go away sooner than his hair grows back. His shaved head makes him look intimidating. You think he did it to project a powerful image?"

"Boomer says so, and it seems to work. No one questions him."

"I won't either because I don't have to attend his status meetings. But I'll keep working on our joint projects. Just don't tell him."

"I won't. He doesn't trust you. He thinks you're faking so you can hold out for more money or do a deal with one of NASA's competitors. There's no evidence, but I hear rumors he can be vindictive enough to track people he doesn't like, so you be careful." "Thanks for telling me. I will, and I'll call as soon as I get settled in LA…"

Electra and Renee kept quietly busy on their own in the SUV for the rest of the day and into the next until Renee began talking about West Texas.

"The videos I watched show how flat the land gets. You can see rows of pumping jacks stretching to the horizon. It's like you're standing in the middle of a shallow bowl. Every way you face, you're looking up at the horizon. And the place is windier and drier than before. Bad dust storms can roll in fast, and it looks like we're driving into one."

"Good thing traffic is light both ways and there's a divide between east and westbound lanes. And just about all the tractor-trailers are self-driving. Their combo software and GPS should make them pretty safe, even in sand and dust storms. But all of us should keep watch." Electra's last words prompted Christi to say,

"Carter and I will watch the sides and rear." Renee said,

"That'll help. I'll handle the front."

The extra eyes helped scan the road and traffic but by early afternoon, buffeting winds and an engulfing, dark-swirling dust cloud forced Electra to drive with headlights on and slow to a crawl. The droning and moaning of the wind blocked out all other exterior sounds; Electra's lightning brain state elevated just in time.

The glaring headlights of a tractor-trailer suddenly beamed directly toward her, but she was ahead of Renee's blood-curdling scream. She swerved onto the right shoulder and accelerated to avoid collision when it rolled over, blocking both lanes. Then she bounced back onto the pavement and zoomed ahead to avoid any collateral damage from the upended truck now ablaze.

But moments later, a second truck did the same, and Electra's lightning reflexes powered the SUV away from disaster. Renee didn't speak until the adrenaline rush had subsided enough for her to say, "That'll never happen to us again. The odds are too—" Christi's words cut her off.

"Some vehicle behind is closing the gap."

Electra was already taking evasive action as soon as she saw the headlights bearing down. She swerved onto the grassy divider strip before slamming on the brakes. The pursuing vehicle sped by; then, after veering onto the eastbound lane, she raced back to the last access ramp and sped away from the Interstate.

After the dust storm blew through, Electra found other roads that took them to an out-of-the-way motel and diner. Enough time had elapsed for both Electra and Renee to decompress, but the events had brought a new topic for Renee.

"If you hadn't been so quick, we could have been killed. Let me show you the document you gave me about God and Religion a while ago. Almost dying brings it to mind."

Renee scrolled it on her laptop.

God and Religion in Your Life

- God and Religion help us understand the world we live in. Some of it we can see; others we can only feel, but in either case they can comfort us.
- There are different religions. Some have one God, others have many. Which one to believe in is a personal choice.
- There are two main types of religions: those of the Eastern Orient, like Buddhism, which is found in China and India, and those of the West. That's where you find Christianity, Judaism, and Islamism.
- Eastern Religions are holistic and cyclic. Each of us is connected to the Universe, and we cycle repeatedly, starting at birth and then growing to reach a peak, and then declining until we die. But we can be happy knowing that we'll be born again.
- Western Religions are different. We are born and grow and decline and die. And when we die, we go to a place called Heaven if God chooses us.
- The Bible gives us a foundation for Western Religions. It is divided into two parts: the Old and New Testaments.
- Old Testament tells us how God created the World. Names you'll hear about: Adam and Eve, Noah, Abraham, Moses, David.
- Important New Testament names: Jesus, the Virgin Mary, Saint Paul. The Apostles.
- Important New Testament beliefs:
- The Trinity of God–God the Father, God the Son (Jesus), and God the Holy Ghost (the experience or feeling we get when God touches our life).
- Jesus lived more than 2,000 years ago and taught people a new way to live (today we call it Christianity). He died to redeem us from our sins. God brought him back to life (resurrected) and he now sits on the right side of God in Heaven.

- We are resurrected from the dead by the Grace of God if we believe in him and lead a righteous life. (Righteous means we follow the Bible's teachings.)

The Catholic Church grew from the seeds of Christianity sown by the Apostles. Catholic church leaders are Priests, Bishops, Cardinals, and Popes. They lead their congregations (believers), teaching and telling them what to believe and do.

Important Historical Events of the Catholic Church:

- In the early 1500s, Martin Luther protested the bad practices of the Catholic Church and which led to the Protestant Reformation and new religions (Protestant religions).
- These religions added new beliefs that sprang up during the Renaissance. (15th and 16th centuries).
- More were added during the Enlightenment (17th to mid-19th centuries). Rationalism and Science sprang to life, and their findings questioned whether God exists. New philosophies emerged because philosophers rejected religious beliefs supported only by Faith or the Pope's Authority. Philosophers placed more importance in each individual (called the "Turn to the Subject"). Religions softened their teachings by emphasizing caring for people (Humanitarianism.) This became the foundation for Modern Religion, which is the handmaiden of Modern Philosophy. (Philosopher Immanuel Kant's efforts to reconcile Faith and Reason become Modern Philosophy's starting point.)
- That worked up to mid-20th century. Two world wars, economic collapses, and the rise of Authoritarian governments put all Western religions into disarray. And ever since then, Christian Religions have become an invitation for people to embark on a personal life journey in which Religion can help heal ourselves by teaching each of us to love one another, especially the victims of our innate lust for power and our desire to dominate the "other".

She waited long enough for Electra to read it before saying,

"When you gave it to me, you said we'd go over it some time. How about now?"

"You don't need me to go over it with you. You've learned and grown so much intellectually I think you know what it says. And there's nothing I want to add to it."

"But what about death? Do you ever think about dying, or what it'll feel like?"

"Everyone does at some point in their life. Let me retrieve a poem I learned long ago that gives a good way of looking at it from different age points of view."

Electra scrolled it, letting Renee read it aloud.

Don't Fear the Reaper
Death should be of less concern the older we become,
Simply one of Nature's Laws when all our work is done.
Something unavoidable that Life will send our way,
Expected then and brings an end to day's soft-setting Sun.
For Youth forsooth it's tragedy,
Death would come too soon,
Their morning star is still in flight to reach a bright high noon.
So sad because it cuts them short with so much yet to say,
Better they should stay awhile and sing out wine-sweet tune.
For those so close to Mid-Life peak, Oh Death is quite unfair,
Much to be accomplished still suspended in the air.
Better for to grant a stay ignore them for awhile,
Returning at a later day when all's been taken care.
But do not fear the Reaper when becoming gray and old,
For those with faith and hope to see what's now emerging bold.
Redemption may await for those on darkling distant isle,
For those who yearn gods grant they learn as Prophets have foretold.

And she spoke again after Renee finished.

"I think you've reached the stage in your education for you to talk more with Indira about these deep, big-picture of Life subjects. Ask her about the modern epic sci-fi fantasy worlds built by J.R.R Tolkien in 'Lord of the Rings,' and C.S. Lewis in 'The Chronicles of Narnia.'

Both of these late 19th to mid-20th century British authors

disliked Modernity's trends and used their books to show other philosophies and ways of living. Tolkien was an atheist, but Lewis converted to Christianity and wrote books like 'Mere Christianity' and 'The Abolition of Man', which coins the term 'men without chests'. That one explains why Christianity serves mankind well even today and criticizes a world that's becoming driven by science and technology without leaving enough room for the most important piece of humanity. It's the piece containing our poetic truth-and-value-driven ethics. By the way, Lewis read 'Mere Christianity' in a series of British radio broadcasts during World War II. However, after today's excitement, I'm too tired to talk about this, so why don't you sleep on it and pick up with Indira when you want?"

"OK, and this is a great way to end the day."

Renee hugged Electra before getting ready for bed. Electra did the same as soon as Renee had tucked in, and she thought herself to sleep, giving thanks for what the day had and hadn't brought.

The new Electra is pretty much ready for action. She and the lightning brain kept disaster away, but today's incidents are too much of a coincidence. Am I being paranoid, or could Zoltan have masterminded the near-collisions and chase? Does he want to kill me or just scare me into giving him what he wants? For the time being, there's no harm in picking Zoltan, especially since I don't have to think about him until I get settled in LA, so it's time to file all this away.

Electra settled into an untroubled sleep.

Chapter 4
October 2171

"California Dreaming...and More"

Electra made a half-day stop in Denver to tell Rich Tabaka and Parson Holsum one part of her emerging plan that needed their human touch. She asked them to add Austin and Washington properties to her growing collection of assets they manage. It already included the Pequot Reservation lab and biotech manufacturing facilities, rare earths mining on other Indian reservations, and recently launched renewable resources businesses in Florida and the Northwest, operated by Indigenous Americans.

Afterward, Electra drove nonstop to LA. She and Renee napped whenever necessary in the SUV while Christi and Carter handled the driving. Speaking only to her alter ego, Alisha took control as soon as Electra stepped into the office picked by Alonzo on the western border of Hollywood.

My dream is coming true. I'm back where I belong, where I fit in, where several lifetimes ago I became the star of my very own Supergirl series before becoming a screenwriter. And my long-ago mentors, Vito Buono and Kathi Lauret, knew I had the goods to strut my stuff.

Electra cut in to keep Alisha in bounds.

Yes, but you had to put Vito in his place when his under-the-table finger play moved into the danger zone during your dinner interview for the role.

Electra paused to let her alter ego continue.

I can still see his wide-eyed look when I shoved the chocolate cake into his mouth without getting a morsel on me.

Alisha waited to hear from Electra.

Your feisty attitude that night got you the part, but don't forget, my obsessive-compulsive drive for fitness powered my athletic career that got us here, first for commercials, and then for your sexy but insouciantly innocent image that commanded the spotlight. And you don't need mentors today. We already have what'll get us noticed, even in this land of beautiful people and talented consultants. Our Tobler-tunnel thigh gap and nickels-holding collarbones will turn heads, as will our Website. Jason's social marketing campaign and then some will make that happen."

Electra waited for Alisha.

And that means I can tone down my appearance. I'll show just enough thigh and cleavage so our clients know we have a lot we're not showing. You let me pick a tony fashion-clothing store, and I'll let the consultant pick clothes, cosmetics, and hairstyles suitable for Alisha, Electra, and Renee. And we'll have clothes for Christi and Carter that fit our 'Consultants to the Stars' image. After all, they'll be our office managers and live in the place.

Electra spoke again.

Well then, I think you should hire an interior designer so the office matches our style. Why not select reproductions of some classic contemporary paintings and let the designer take it from there?

Alisha replied,

I'm ahead of you on that score. I've already picked 'Mystery and Melancholy of a Street' by Georgio de Chirico, 'Nude Descending Staircase' by Marcel Duchamp, 'Water Lilies' by Claude Monet, and 'The Kiss' by Constantin Brancusi. And we'll have a copy of his polished brass sculpture 'Bird in Space' that people will see as soon as they walk in. So, while I'm doing this, why don't you and Renee find us a place to live and more things for us to do?

Electra agreed, saying,

Good idea, but let me offer a suggestion. Because our clientele will skew toward women, why not match each painting with one done by a female artist active at the same time and in that style? There are many who never got the recognition they deserved until much later.

Alisha wrapped up their chat by saying,

Excellent. You and I can spin enchanting stories for how our services fit each client. So, let's get busy.

Electra spent a day refreshing her memory of Los Angeles by driving around the town while Renee surfed the Internet to help find places to live. Electra spoke while driving to give her partner some guidelines.

"LA's the entertainment capital of the world, and our office is ideally located for making the most of our consulting opportunity. But the city's so spread out; it's like a collection of distinctive small towns and neighborhoods, so we have plenty to choose from. Alonzo booked us into the Sky Boutique Hotel, which is between the office and Hollywood, so we better look farther west."

Renee kept busy surfing until she spoke fifteen minutes later.

"Let me read you an article about where actors should live in LA. It says there are three main areas, Central Los Angeles, the San Fernando Valley, which is aka the Valley, and West Los Angeles. All are safe and have lots of neat features, but they're expensive. And it says West LA costs the most."

Renee waited for Electra.

"What else does it say about West LA?"

"It's the most well-known area in the whole city, with lots of beaches and celebrities. Here are some of the places it mentions, Santa Monica, Palms, Mar Vista, Playa Del Rey, and Pico-Robertson. Whatcha think?"

Electra tapped into her memory before saying,

"Santa Monica sounds good. We'll be close to beaches as well as potential clients. And I'll find a designer who can recommend places to rent. Let's drive around it."

They cruised through for the next ninety minutes, passing among other places the Santa Monica Pier and a tourist district holding an iconic "End of Route 66" plaque. Electra pointed out the beach activities, which included volleyball and surfing, before returning to the hotel restaurant.

Electra could see from Renee's expression that the tour had overwhelmed her, so she did most of the talking.

"We saw a lot of good-looking, athletic-minded young people. You'll fit right in and make new friends, and it'll be a welcome change of pace from our consulting work."

"You think I can handle both?"

"Sure, you can. And I can find the right designer to get us started." Electra and Renee worked at the office during the next week. Renee took charge of getting the androids acclimated while Electra split her time between finding a decorator and finding a way to introduce herself to the Scripps Institute. She used Alonzo's consulting office contact for the first and Britt for the second. By the end of the month, she had arranged a Saturday morning designer meeting, which might also give her more information to help convince Scripps.

There were actually two parts. The first consisted of a paleontologist's lecture Renee had found at the La Brea Tar Pit Museum. Electra picked out some of the facts Renee talked about afterward that she could use at her Scripps interview.

"No wonder earthquakes threaten the West Coast. There's a thousand-mile crack in the ocean floor only eighty miles offshore, and it adds to the risks caused by LA's San Andreas Fault. The speaker said it could cause gigantic earthquakes and tidal waves that'd wipe out a lot of the Pacific Northwest forests. It's happened many times before, and when it does it causes regional climate change. What did he call it?"

"A tectonic plate rift named the Cascadia Subduction Zone that erupts upward when the pressure gets too great. And how did you like what he said about the tar pits?"

"I did. And although now they're only a couple of inches deep, they've been there for thousands of years and were deep enough to trap animals and humans who wandered in. That's where the Museum's fossils come from. Do we have time to walk through it?" "Not on this visit. We have to leave for the Los Angeles County Museum of Art to meet our designer. Lucky for us it's close enough to walk. And isn't it nice the sun usually shines here in October?"

"I guess so."

"Hey, cheer up. You'll like living here once we settle in. And maybe the designer can recommend the right place to live."

Electra liked the designer, who worked full-time at the Museum of Art, setting up displays or renovating galleries, and Renee did too after she said how good both of them looked.

"After I pick your office color scheme, I know a couple of fashion boutiques that'll pick the right clothes for both of you. But tell me first, what image do you want to project?"

"Our consulting business is called Trans-Astro Consulting Services, and our tagline is AI-Empowerment for the Stars."

"What services do you provide?"

"A full range that Hollywood females should like. Among them are investing, life coaching, beauty, life styling, and entertainment, all using the latest artificial intelligence enhancements. I think our image should be a combination of high-tech and Hollywood glamour, and I've already told you what reproductions and sculpture I want to use, so why don't you take it from here?"

When the designer ended the meeting ninety minutes later, Electra added a final comment.

"Thanks for the name and address of the fashion store. We'll go there after we've found a place in Santa Monica to live. You wouldn't, by any chance, know someone who could recommend a place, would you?"

"Timing's everything. I bought a two-bedroom unit in Santa Monica's Sunset View townhome development, and I can vouch for its quality and location. And it just so happens that another owner wants to sublet hers because she's going to work in Bollywood for the next couple of years. Why don't I introduce you to her?"

"If we can meet her today, I'll treat all four of us to a late lunch or early dinner, whichever she prefers."

"I'll call right now."

Electra's serendipitous timing held. By the time they finished dinner, she had signed the agreement for a tony-furnished two-bedroom townhome she and Renee would move into during the third weekend of November. And she resisted the urge to shop on Sunday for clothes until the flush of today's successful meetings subsided.

Electra used Monday and Tuesday to prepare for her upcoming Scripps meeting, which would be 1 p.m. Monday of next week. She gave Renee the assignment of researching via the Web Woods Hole and Scripps Oceanographic Centers, and while Renee was doing that, Electra was searching the recesses of her memory,

Scripps should remember that Irani assisted Jonathan on their NASA-related projects, and I can tie it in with the Arctic climate change projects we did with Woods Hole. And if that's not enough, I'll mention the Great Barrier Reef expedition. All I have to do is remember enough now so I can fill in the gaps later.

Electra felt good enough by Friday to relax on Saturday by shopping for clothes. Not only did she come away with stylish outfits for all three, Electra, Alisha, and Renee, but also with new hairstyles and makeup, which highlighted her minimal jewelry, the gold lightning bolt earrings, and medallion mounted on a black velvet choker.

Electra noticed that even though Renee didn't say so, she

liked the results, especially how the cosmetics gave just the right shading to her cheek markings, so she complimented her on the drive back to the hotel.

"The people at Scripps will say we look like a team of research professionals, and you can speak at the interview when I ask you to tell them more."

"About what? What should I practice?"

"About the Amazon Rainforest climate change, you saw there. And you can talk about collecting samples and the work we did, recording climate change-related coral population variations at the Great Barrier Reef. You have all day tomorrow to review, and please don't overthink. Just go with your memory. And you can rehearse Monday morning while I drive."

"Thanks to you, I know what to do."

"I do too. We'll do fine, so please, rest easy."

Serendipity continued smiling on the pair during Monday morning's two-hour, one-hundred-and-twenty-mile drive to San Diego, but once there they didn't need any help. Their preparation covered all the questions asked, and the interviewers had already vetted her, using the references provided on her application. Most of the interview became simply a matter of Electra's accepting the terms of her research position, for which she could combine her independent work with what Scripps had in mind.

Renee picked the snack stop on the drive back, elated with the compliments that had come her way. Both she and Electra enjoyed sharing quiet time for the rest of the drive home, but Alisha got in one more comment for Electra.

Everything's in place for our California dream to become even more than we thought. I'm sure you'll keep Renee busy on Scripps projects, but we should hire a young fellow to work with me on the others, which should attract a lot of Hollywood-type females.

To which Electra replied,

I like that idea. Perhaps you can find candidates online, or better yet, while you and Renee are prowling around the leisure scene.

Alisha preferred a different word.

Please don't make me sound so predatory. My standards are as high as yours once I include my fun factor, so Renee and I will be canvassing the leisure scene.

I apologize. Please proceed and ask for my help if you need it.

I will, but I won't.

Electra decided not to reply. With or without words, she and her alter ego always understood each other.

Chapter 5
December 2171

"Hollywood Holidays"

Electra and Renee worked diligently up to the Thanksgiving weekend, and knowing all about Hollywood restaurants, Alisha made reservations for Thanksgiving at the Barish, located in the Roosevelt Hollywood Hotel. She and Renee picked their way through the Holiday Buffet, making sure to save enough room for desserts while enjoying the plush ambience of the interior and the guests. The diners enjoyed eyeing them as well because the duo dressed up for the occasion. Even in this setting, Electra and Renee turned heads.

They enjoyed sightseeing the weekend afterward, visiting tourist attractions according to Renee's agenda, which would minimize distance and exertion and maximize viewing pleasure that the weather made superb. They started at the Hollywood Walk of Fame, a five-block stretch of 2800 embedded stars on Hollywood Boulevard, followed by a tour of the Academy of Motion Picture Museum, and after a snack they window shopped along Rodeo Drive before driving through Hollywood's rich and famous residential area and then ending at Griffith Park Observatory for a commanding view of the sun setting over LA below.

Refreshed by the change of pace, both made fine progress the following week. Jason's social media campaign generated an increasing number of online client requests, which Christi and Renee converted into actual clients or scheduled for personal visits that Alisha would handle. Meanwhile, Alisha screened candidates for her consulting associate position, finding several who would fit but not making a decision.

Alisha decided that she and Renee needed to explore more of the Santa Monica Boardwalk and would do so on roller skates, using the mid-December Saturday that had picture-perfect weather. When she told the skate rental guy this would be their first time, he gave them preferential treatment by helping them lace up before guiding them through basic skating techniques. Alisha noticed he gave Renee special attention.

Soon they were skating among those enjoying an early afternoon session of roller skating and blading, sidewalk surfing, biking, or walking. Alisha made most of the comments. Renee listened while absorbing all she saw.

"Lots of volleyball teams out here today; lots of surfers heading to and from the beach, and lots of guys and gals using the exercise stations. Maybe we'll stop and do some pullups. How many do yoouu—" Alisha never finished her words. Two rollerbladers whizzed by, knocking her down.

By the time Renee finished picking her up, the offenders had returned, and the bigger started badmouthing them.

"You damn tourists better get outta the way if you can't skate straight. Leave the place to those who know what to do." His partner added to the insult by pushing them off the pavement, but before the bullies could do more, help came from a sidewalk surfer, who used his board as a cattle prod, pushing them down and out of the way.

"Hey, watch your mouth or I'll do more than push." The bullies decided they were no match for their taller and more muscular opponent, especially since their rollerblades hampered fighting mobility, so they skated away, saying nothing and leaving space for Alisha to step in.

"Well, those two won't head back anytime soon to bother us. We're Alisha and Renee Kirchner. And who can we thank for helping?"

A female skateboarder zoomed to a stop next to him before he replied.

"My name's Kai Wailani, and this is my kid sister Kaila."

"We've skated enough to get thirsty. If you'll pick the place, I'll be happy to treat all of us."

"Kaila's here more than me. Let's let her lead the way."

Alisha studied from the rear as the foursome glided toward an umbrella-covered roundtable.

Their looks match what have to be Native Hawaiian names, *dark hair and complexion on attractive features. And what a kid sister. She's toned and tanned and as tall as me but with a little more muscle mass in all the right places. And he's a couple of inches taller but with a touch more muscle. I'll prime the conversation, then just sit back and see where it goes. And I hope Renee joins in.*

Alisha did that after the drinks arrived ten minutes later.

"We recently moved here from DC to start my LA Life Coach Consulting business. Renee's my research assistant. I bet you're Native Hawaiians. Have you been here long?"

"About eight years. I came from Honolulu to go to UCLA and graduated four years ago with a degree in Sports Physiology. Kaila came the year I graduated and might graduate next year if surfing doesn't get in the way."

Kai's words prompted Renee to say,

"Isn't surfing Hawaii's national sport? Didn't you invent it?" Kaili answered before her brother.

"Cave paintings show that Polynesians invented it, but they brought it when they settled in Hawaii. It's been our national sport ever since."

"So, why does it get in the way?" Kai cut in.

"She wants to be a pro surfer, like our Dad, who died in a surfing accident, but the competition's tough in Hawaii, so the family told her to follow me to UCLA and surf in LA while getting a degree. And—" Kaila cut Kai off.

"And I'm doing both, spending enough time on each. And like your mother guessed, we're Native Hawaiian through and through. Our first and last names are related to water and oceans, so you might say surfing's in our DNA. What's in yours?"

Alisha saw Renee struggling to come up with an answer, so she said,

"Renee grew up in the Amazon Rainforest, and I brought her to live with me. She's like the daughter I never had. Do you play volleyball in addition to surfing? Perhaps you could teach and introduce her to some in the younger crowd. And I'll be happy to pay for your time and expertise."

Kai said,

"We'll both do the teaching. My fitness club job doesn't give me enough to do."

Alisha decided to end this part of the conversation.

"Let's swap phone numbers. I'll call to set up our first surfing lesson after checking my calendar. Now, please tell me about your B.S. in sports physiology…"

Alisha called Kai that evening, and they picked Monday for the first surfing lesson. Kai would supply wet suits and surfboards, and when the van rolled up at 10 a.m., Kai yelled through the passenger's window,

"Kaila's driving because her van can hold all the gear. I'll climb out and give you your wetsuits so you can change into them before we go." The van rolled on twenty minutes later. This time, Kaila did the talking.

"I've got scads of beaches to choose from, but I chose Santa Monica's Point Break location because it's close. We'll be on the beach soon. And I checked today's surf conditions. The sun and waves are perfect for your first lesson."

Renee's voice registered her growing excitement. "What'll we do first?"

"Carry stuff to the beach and let Kai explain when we get there." Kai continued a half-hour later while lying on his surfboard. "Everyone, watch me show you how to paddle. Lay on the board like me with feet on the tail and arms over the side rails. Then paddle like I'm doing."

Kai called a halt after ten minutes of giving corrections or compliments.

"OK, everyone up and watch Kaila show you how to get up and stand on the surfboard."

Kaila's agility added to her words. Five minutes of practice later, Kai gave the next command.

"Now we'll actually do this in the surf. Renee teams with Kaila and Alisha with me. Don't be surprised by how cold the water is, but you'll find it refreshing after awhile. We'll paddle past the tiny breakers, then we'll show you how to catch a wave. And then it's up to you to stand and surf."

Alisha's fitness helped her do everything right away but actually surf. Kai had to give her one-on-one assistance nearly ten times until she caught on. After that, all he had to do was admire his agile student.

Renee learned even faster; she caught the first wave and after that kept going all the way to shore before paddling back for more. Kaila surfed alongside her for the next hour before they joined the other team on the beach towel.

Kaila chatted gaily after drying her hair.

"Renee's a natural. She popped up and kept going and going.

Surfing must be in her genes too."

Compliments continued from all and overcame Renee's reluctance to talk in a group.

"You're a great teacher, and I practiced years ago surfing on the Amazon."

Kai's surprised voice cut in before she could say more." "You mean you rode the Pororoca Tidal Bore?"

"Uh, what's that?"

"It's supposed to be the longest wave in the world. It travels hundreds of miles on the Amazon through the rainforest and can be up to a ten-foot wall of water moving close to thirty mph. And it's a dangerous ride. Surfers have been swept into the Forest and never seen again."

Alisha saw an opportunity to add something from Electra.

"I'll bet the name comes from a tribal word meaning loud roar, and it's caused by lunar and solar alignment during high tides. But no matter, you sure impressed us."

Kai used the last words as a segue to say,

"That'll end our first lesson. Let's get out of our wet suits and get something to eat."

He and Kaila showed Renee how to surround Alisha with a private space of blankets for stripping naked and putting on dry clothes. She thought to herself when doing.

The sun on bare skin is such a primal pleasure. I could lay in it for hours. And Kai's glancing away is so civilized. He's just added to what I'm looking for.

After everyone had changed, Alisha spoke while the group carried all the gear to the van.

"Why not pick a sit-down place in Santa Monica," to which Kaila said,

"I know where we'll go. I want to introduce Renee to some of my surfer friends."

Several booths said hi to her as a server showed the foursome to a booth, and after placing orders, Kaila and Renee joined a group at another one. After redirecting the server to that location, Alisha had Kai all to herself.

After just the right amount of small talk, she said,

"Your education and work background fit what I need, and you certainly have the people skills to work for me as a life coach consultant. You'll earn more, learn more, and certainly enjoy more with me than where you are now. Would you like to discuss this further at our office on Wednesday?"

"I sure would. And I guarantee that I'm as good in the gym or an office as I am in the water."

"I believe you. Well, that's enough business talk. Let's finish eating and order a dessert…"

Brother and sister arrived at 9 a.m. Alisha introduced them to the androids before giving a tour and then let the girls chat while she started the meeting with Kai in her office with the door closed.

"Let me show you our home page."

Kai studied it for a minute before she continued.

Trans-Astro Consulting Services
"AI-Empowerment for the Stars"

We provide ChatGPT GUI Interfaces for:

- Astro-Investing: AI-Empowered Portfolio Management that matches Your Goals
- Life Coaching: Goal-Centered Meditative Counseling
- Lightning-Bolt Gaming: Beyond State-of-The-Art Gambling Platform
- AI-Artistry: Virtual Reality Enhancements to Your Audio-Visual Image
- Age-Beauty Lifestyling: Nutrition and Exercise for Age- Deceleration
- AI-Empowered Entertainment: Novels and Screenwriting Development

Click on Each Bullet for more details.

Click here for Introductory Video: _____

YOU are the Star in Your Singular Universe. Please contact us when You are ready to shine.

"You can click on the bullets later. I launched our Social Media marketing campaign a month ago, which directs our target clients to this page. What do you think our target is?"

"I'd say both men and women working in Hollywood who are early to mid-career. And this portfolio of services has something for everyone."

"Yes, and my market research indicates we'll attract more females than males. I expect most clients will sign up using our ChatGPT interface, but those who need the personal touch will leave a name and phone number for us to call back. And that's where you fit in. In addition to running the office and supervising Christi and Carter, for which Renee will assist, you'll follow up on the messages left, keeping track of those who would like to visit with me in the office or at their homes. And once you feel comfortable with our routine, you can do the in-person follow-up. Any questions?"

"Only one, when do I start?"

"First week in January. And now let's talk about salary and benefits. I think they'll be to your liking as well."

Electra ended the meeting an hour later by adding a starting assignment.

"Between now and your starting, please do some phone-call role playing with Renee. And please keep track of Renee's surfing lessons so we can pay Kaila."

"Will you be included?"

"No, one lesson was enough. And I hope Renee and Kaila become friends."

"I think they already are. They can team up in volleyball too."

"Well, I look forward to being at that first practice session. Now let's celebrate by going out to lunch."

Renee and Kaila joined them and seemed just as pleased. They would talk later to arrange more lessons, and that night, Renee confided to Alisha,

"I feel better and better about being in LA. Thanks for all you're doing for me."

"Please remember what I already said. You're the daughter I've always wanted..."

Renee and Alisha kept busy running the office for the rest of the week, and on Friday, Alisha arranged a Saturday visit to a potential client named Marne-Anne Dionne, a late-thirties actress-turned screenwriter who lives in West Hollywood. Renee scoped out the area via the Web the night before.

"According to this blurb, West Hollywood is famous for being the home of the Sunset Strip and LA's LGBT community. The city has a neighborhood feel, a mix of owners and renters, plenty of nightlife, shopping, dining, and fun. Its central location--bordering Beverly Hills, Hollywood Hills, and Hollywood--makes it a hub of activity that draws many locals and tourists alike. Take a look at the photos." Seconds later, Alisha said,

"If she looks as good as what you're showing me, I'll do my best to get her. I've practiced my pitch and tomorrow I get to throw it." Marne and her house looked even better. Her dark complexion and long black hair stood out against the sparkling white, low-cut pants suit, and Alisha liked her direct manner when talking about her background.

"I started in daytime soaps and moved into online streaming videos before getting supporting roles in movies. But my success led to divorce, and I haven't remarried. I've got one mid-twenties son, and I hope screenwriting will extend my career when my looks fade. Maybe your coaching can help."

"I think it will. Let me show you my life coaching philosophy." Electra placed her laptop on Marne's lap after bringing up the right page.

Trans-Astro Consulting Services
"AI-Empowerment for the Stars"
Life Coaching Philosophy for Clients

My Philosophy: A Neuroscience-extended synthesis of Eastern (Cyclic/Holistic) and Western (Linear/Goal-Driven) Philosophies combined with the Psychology of Flow (Immersive Focus in the Moment)
Neuroscience Says:

- Purpose of Life/Existence for all Organisms: Survive long enough to pass genes to next generation. Requires Primal Instincts for Physiological and Sexual Needs.
- Human Evolution created Cognition/Emotion/Feeling that added to Life's Purpose Caring/Compassion for Tribal Members. Love Emerges From/Transcends Caring/Compassion
- Cultural Evolution redefines Purpose of Life as Empathetic Caring/Compassion/Sharing with Others, which translates to: The Purpose of Life is to find

Meaning via Empathetic Attention to Others, which condenses to: The Purpose of Life is to find Happiness (Happiness leads to Empathetic Attention and vice versa; Happiness is greater than Mere Pleasure).

How to Achieve Happiness:

- Happiness is contentment achieved by a State of Mind and not determined by External Events.
- Appreciate What You Have rather than focusing on obtaining All That You Want.
- "Know Thyself," Your Self-Worth, and Overarching Objective Ethical Values Granting Each Person the Rights to Life, Liberty, Pursuit of Happiness. Note Distinctions Between Non-Rights of Democracy/Majority and Equality/Identity.
- Be realistic in setting Goals and Expectations.
- Use Active Cognition/Meditation/Immersive Flow to strive for Happiness.

What we get from the Effort:

- Better Health, Professional Career, and Personal Relationships; Longer Life.
- Ability to deal better with Pain and Loss.
- A more Adaptive Mind for Overcoming Obstacles by achieving a Balanced Life.
- Reduced Levels of Anger, Stress, Anxiety, Guilt, and Hatred.
- Better Understanding of Truth and Honesty; More Appreciation for the Finiteness of Life and How Precious Each Person is.

Connections to Religion:

- Extends the Buddha's Three Teachings: Life is Difficult/Painful; Pain/Suffering lead to Growth; Growth leads us closer and closer to Nirvana (A transcendent state in which there is neither suffering, desire, nor sense of self, and the subject is released from the effects of karma and the cycle of death and rebirth.)

- Incorporates many teachings of Jesus.

ALL THIS LEADS TO A SPIRITUAL LIFE INDEPENDENT OF FORMAL, ORGANIZED RELIGION.

Alisha talked as Marne worked her way down the page.

"I've studied enough religion and philosophy as well as the hard and soft sciences to build a positive, pragmatic approach to life that rewards our cognitive, emotional, and physical personas by taking the right steps to achieve happiness. We each should do our best by taking control, setting realistic goals, and appreciating what we have."

Then she waited until Marne said,

"I like this. It fits no matter the race, religion, creed, or color. Please tell me more about your services."

Alisha brought up the home page and then clicked through all the dropdowns, providing just enough detail to maintain a dialogue.

Trans-Astro Consulting Services
"AI-Empowerment for the Stars"

We provide ChatGPT GUI Interfaces for:

- **Astro-Investing: AI-Empowered Portfolio Management that matches Your Goals**
- **Life Coaching: Goal-Centered Meditative Counseling**
- **Lightning-Bolt Gaming: Beyond State-of-The-Art Gambling Platform**
- **AI-Artistry: Virtual Reality Enhancements to Your Audio-Visual Image**
- **Age-Beauty Lifestyling: Nutrition and Exercise for Age- Deceleration**
- **AI-Empowered Entertainment: Novels and Screenwriting Development**

Click on Each Bullet for more details.
Click here for Introductory Video: _____
YOU are the Star in Your Singular Universe. Please contact us when You are ready to shine.

Marne ended the meeting forty-five minutes later.

"I like what I see. How about we start in January with the Age- Beauty and Screenwriting Development pieces?"

"Perfect, and you decide if you'd like to meet back here or in my office."

"We'll do that later, but if you're available, I'd like you to come to my Holiday open house."

"Just tell me the date and time, and I'll be there. May I bring my partner, Renee?"

"Is she old enough to drink?"

"She's 21, and I guarantee she's mature beyond her years."

"Well then, I'll see you back here on Saturday, the 28th, anytime after 6 p.m."

"Thanks for the invite, and even more for becoming my client…" Electra prepared her traditional Christmas Eve dinner of baked beans and Swedish meatballs and then relaxed with Renee while watching a recent Dickens Christmas Carol movie. Christmas Day was equally low-key, as were the days leading up to Marne's open house, for which she and Renee dressed to fit the occasion.

Alisha explained to Renee while driving what to expect.

"Stay next to me and look and listen like you normally do while I chat with as many guests as I can to find out which might be potential clients. And remember to smile while answering any questions they send your way."

"What should I drink?"

"You'll be fine if follow me; stay with Champagne and nibble on the hors d'oeuvres."

Alisha realized she had impressed Marne because she made a special effort to introduce her life coach to a number of guests, and when Alisha redirected the conversation to each, they wanted her to call them so they could learn more about her business. She impressed all of them by using her lightning brain to memorize names and addresses and not handing out business cards.

Electra planned to spend New Year's Eve at home engaged in her traditional activity of planning what she would do for the entire year, but this time she would focus on only the next month and let results dictate what she would do after that. And she was pleased when Kaila invited Renee to a New Year's Eve party.

After Kaila picked her up, she sat on the sofa, watching the Times Square Ball Drop while listening to herself.

Now that our LA office is up and running, I'll let Kai and Renee take charge while I go back to DC. I have to find out how my East Coast consulting business is doing, so I'll call Alonzo tomorrow to plan my January agenda. And no matter what I find out, me and my Lightning Brain will handle whatever develops.

General Horatio Goodman had more important matters to look at than watching a New Year's Eve ball drop somewhere. That's why he ordered Zoltan to meet with him in the Oval Office. They were watching New Year's Eve news broadcasts recapping the year and projecting the next. Putting the monitor on mute after one show ended, he asked Zoltan for recommendations.

"You have to pick a party that'll nominate you for President, and then you better let me put together your platform team. You better practice more for your televised presentation that comes on before the first college football playoff game."

"Tell me again the major talking points you've put in it."

"You have to assure the people that you'll make sure technology works for them, and that our domestic programs will make life better. And you have to defuse growing concerns about a bogus international conspiracy out to rule the world."

Horatio rubbed his chin before saying,

"I can do that. And how are you doing with all those NASA projects? Did you find a replacement for that researcher who came down with migraines?"

"I'm still looking into that, but not to worry. One way or another, I'll keep track of her "

Chapter 6
January 2172

"A Too-Full Schedule Ahead"

The freakish weather hitting up and down the East Coast delayed the landing of Electra and Alonzo's Sunday, January 4th flight to DC; the thundersnow storm that greeted her gave a reminder that the climate change issue won't go away, but it might also help convince some of the people she planned to meet to join forces on upcoming projects.

China had supper on the table soon after Electra arrived at her house. A casual chat after dinner would be their Washington Projects status meeting. After China said that Alonzo and the androids freed up her time for delving faster into her assignments, Electra dug into the details.

"How do Washington and the public like acting-President Goodman and his Chief of Staff Zoltan Sultani?"

"According to polls, both give a thumbs-up on the General and think he'll use the Democratic Party to run for re-election because its domestic and foreign policies jibe with what both the public and allies want, but they give question marks on Sultani. On one hand, they like his direct approach, although he can sometimes be too blunt, but the rumors that he's too soft on that phantom Bigger Brother Conspiracy linger. I've done enough digging to agree but haven't uncovered any links. How about you?"

"I've been too busy setting up the LA office to think about it. If I make some useful political contacts out there, I'll let you know."

"I'll bet you'll make some. Hollywood's reality likes to combine plots with politics. Haven't there been a lot of actors and actresses who've become respected politicians?"

"Many, but it was unusual in the early days. However, here's a famous example. Shirley Temple was the highest-grossing box-office star at the age of five, and her popularity saved the

Fox Studio from going under in 1932. She went on to become the most famous child actress of all time, but she quit when only twenty-two to seek a career in politics. She never got elected to Congress, but her working for the League of Women Voters and President Nixon's campaign eventually got her appointed positions in the UN and ambassador to an African country and then to one in Europe. Quite a success story."

"It certainly is. Have you seen any of her movies?"

"My favorites are 'Heidi' and 'Rebecca of Sunnybrook Farm,' and she could sing and dance as well as act. When you watched, she seemed to have the brain of an exceptional adult."

"Did she have a normal childhood? Lots of kid stars in entertainment or sports didn't."

"Psychologists say that child prodigies seldom have normal childhoods. I read a little of her bio, and it says that aside from the awful punishments and pressure, she also had to endure sexual harassment from producers. I can understand why she quit when she did. Her Hollywood experiences trained her to handle politics."

"I think you're right. She could have set up and run a DC consulting business. But no matter, I'd still prefer working for you."

"Thanks for your vote of confidence. Now please tell me about Connecticut Congressman Benjamin Chaska, our Pequot Indian leader Feather Trueson, and the status of the Native American Indian Alliance..."

China talked for a half-hour before Electra interrupted the monologue.

"I've heard enough; you're on target. I'll follow up with Feather and let you know what we'll do next. I think I'll go to bed early so I'm ready for tomorrow, but let me help do the kitchen cleanup first. And why don't you work at home? That way, Alonzo and I will have the office all to ourselves."

"Thanks, that'll save me the trouble of driving if this lousy weather sticks around..."

Neither Monday morning's sleet nor snow could keep Alonzo from driving Electra to the office. They stopped en route to pick up some muffins and doughnuts, and when they added a couple of cans of Coke, the mood inside the conference room beat that outside. During the drive, she had already complimented him regarding his LA office choice, so she shifted topics.

"You've talked with RT and PH before. Please call them this month to have them help you manage all East Coast properties. Other than this week, I don't have trip details yet, but my upcoming schedule will keep you busy."

"Where will we be going if the weather cooperates?"

"We'll start driving on Wednesday to the Pequot Lab, stopping first at the Woods Hole Oceanic Institute. But before that, I'd like us to meet with Professor Plannert at his GWU office. I'm his Environmental Scanning Committee consultant. He might have something for us to check out."

"OK, and what about today?"

"Instead of visiting in person, please set up an online meeting with Monet."

Monet appeared on the monitor ten minutes later and spoke first. "I'm pleased you decided to call rather than drive here. Alonzo will take care of the mood elevators I brought. Now, what is your first topic?"

"Anything new internationally regarding Kinslinger or a link to the Bigger Bro conspiracy?"

"No, but my contacts think General Goodman better run for office. They expect him to choose the Democratic Party. It's the most reasonable of the four."

"Mine do too, and what about Feather Trueson's Native American Indian Alliance? How's that going?"

"You must help her with the Indigenous Peoples Worldwide Alliance piece. It is growing beyond her capabilities. Darla wants to include some African tribes, and China's aggressiveness worries the Polynesian Island community. I think there are other indigenous people in the Middle East and India that feel the same way."

Alonzo listened as the two females traded ideas for the next hour, and he spoke as soon as Electra ended the call.

"Good thing I've already checked. Our passports don't need renewing for a couple of years."

"We won't need them where we're going for lunch. And when we get back, let's call Eve…"

Eve answered immediately when Electra called two hours

later, using her cell phone.

"I knew you wouldn't want to drive. How are you?" "Doing fine, thanks to Alonzo. How about you and Nari?"

"I'm sorry we forgot to bring you into our New Year's Eve conference call with Nila and Sanjay. We'll do better next time. How's your LA consulting business?"

"Renee and I have it humming along. I might have some clients for you to chat with regarding holistic exercising and nutritional supplements. We can—" Eve's enthusiasm bubbled over what Electra never got a chance to say.

"That reminds me. Do you ever watch some of those videos showing some guy in a white coat bragging about how smart he is because he just came up with an herbal pill that'll save your life by overcoming the brain killers lurking in whatever you're eating or curing the ringing in your ears that's doing the same? I do, but I've never researched which ones work and why and how to combine them. You're great at researching things. Maybe you could do that and put together a snazzy online ad for our Websites. Whatcha think?"

"Uh, that's a good idea. I'll put that on my to-do list. Now, please tell me more about you and Nari and your Mumbai connection." Alonzo joined the ensuing conversation, which ended ninety minutes later. Afterward, he said,

"Sis never runs out of words. I'm glad we called after lunch rather than before."

"Me too. She wore out my ears. Let's adjourn and recharge for tomorrow."

Tuesday's meeting in Professor Plannert's office began as pleasantly as the morning's weather. After his always cordial greeting, he asked his first question, which Alonzo answered.

"I'm her logistics and security coordinator; I found the place in LA for her office."

Electra picked up from there.

"And from there I found a place to live and then connected with the Scripps Institute. They offered me a visiting researcher position." Electra paused for Plannert's reaction.

"Good for you and Scripps too. According to one of my committee members, Scripps wants to link the Mars Mission climate data to Earth's for assessing the interplay between Earth's oceans and atmospheres, and how that affects the ecological balance between plants and animals. That's what her graduate students are researching. Do you know what that might be?"

"No, what did she tell you?"

"Wind and ocean currents affect each other. She said that even though some glaciers are melting because of warm ocean currents, others are growing because of colder regional winds. Melting glaciers bring in plants first and then marine and animal species, while those forming do just the opposite. She told me that NASA satellites can track changes in Antarctic penguin guano and use it as a proxy for climate change. And they can do the same by tracking the elapsed time of albatrosses circling the globe to measure long-term changes in high-altitude airflow. If you have the time, maybe you could connect her to NASA."

"I'll try, and perhaps I can connect her to Scripps or Woods Hole. Alonzo and I will stop there tomorrow on our drive that way."

"And on your next visit, could you give an informal lecture to my Committee about a philosophical foundation that people doing STEM-type research would find helpful? You are so good giving such talks."

"I'll try putting it together."

"Excellent, and now, please tell me more about your LA consulting business."

An hour later, Electra ended the meeting. Just before leaving, she said,

"I'm splitting my time working between LA and DC, so I'll call before I come back, and you can let your Committee know the latest..."

Electra used the drive time to explain why they would stop at Woods Hole.

"This will be my first visit to Cape Cod, but Irani assisted on a couple of projects coordinated by marine biologists Bob and Marlene Rodenbaugh. I've never met them, but they might be interested in my Scripps Institute projects. Do you know what cephalopods are?" "My NAVY SEAL training didn't include much about marine biology. Tell me."

"There are four major species of these sea creatures—octopus, squid, cuttlefish, and nautilus. Studies have shown they're the smartest invertebrates. I've watched videos showing their amazing feats, like opening jars to eat the fish inside or covering up with shells to hide from sharks. Their brain's distributed among all the tentacles, and their astounding biochemistry and DNA make them valuable for bio-drug development."

"What did Irani do?"

"I don't know the details. We'll have to let the Rodenbaughs tell us at the restaurant they picked for dinner."

Electra let the host take them to the Rodenbaugh's table, even though she knew what they looked like. Alisha's acting ability helped Electra introduce themselves and pretend a first meeting. She knew they would like Alonzo, and as dinner moved along, so did the details of Electra's trip as well as the work the Rodenbaugh's had done with Irani. Electra listened to them, but concentrated more on her internal voice.

They're bringing back my pre-NASA memories of Jonathan Segal, and how Irani met him at a Professor Plannert committee meeting. He was so assertive professionally and so shy sexually, but we worked around that. And he's the guy who introduced me to my octopi pets, Electra and Thaumas. I saved them from a shark attack, and they saved me from a speargun-toting bad guy.

Jonathan's also the guy who introduced me to NASA. I came close to forming a family with him and Renee, but I think it was Bigger-Bro who got in the way and faked his hit-and-run death ... OK, that's enough reminiscing. Now let's get back to the present.

By the time everyone had a second after-dinner drink, the Rodenbaughs had agreed to participate with Scripps and NASA on any climate change or oceanographic projects Electra might cobble together. And she let Alonzo end the conversation.

"I'm Electra's logistics and security coordinator, so you can depend on me to take care any of those problems. If I'd been around a couple of years ago, maybe Jonathan's office at GWU wouldn't have been trashed. But going forward, I can handle any bad guys coming our way on land, sea, or air. My SEAL training will come into play. But let's hope I won't need to. And I'm pretty sure I won't need to for the rest of this trip. We're driving tomorrow to the Pequot Reservation."

Mentioning the Reservation prompted Marlene to say,

"Jonathan told me about the octopus tank Irani had there.

Too bad her house burned down when she was in it. Well, maybe Electra can extend her legacy."

Electra ended the conversation.

"Perhaps I can. I'll do my best with the help of her friends…"

While driving to the nearby motel, Alonzo asked about the upcoming schedule.

"Where are we headed tomorrow?"

"We'll visit Feather Trueson mid-morning, and afterward go to the Deus Lab."

"You're the boss, but I got a question. Trueson and the Deus Lab are near Stonington, Connecticut, and we drove past it to get here. Why didn't we stop there first and go to Cape Cod afterward? Woods Hole is only 120 miles farther."

"I'm using a sales-call route planning technique I learned long ago. Suppose you're a sales rep that has a geographically defined territory. Locate your home office on the map; then draw five lines radiating outward. Each line represents a day of the work week. And on each line, you plot the sales calls you'll make. You follow what I'm saying so far?"

"I get it. You space the lines so they're all the same number of degrees apart, and the rep starts his day by driving to the farthest location on that radius. That way, every call takes them closer to home, which always feels good."

"That's the idea. And we can decide when we're ready to leave the Lab if we want to drive back to DC or stop somewhere along the way."

"Not a problem. Either way, I'm ready for whatever comes up…" Electra and Alonzo sat across from Feather at her office the next morning. Electra guided the conversation after introducing Alonzo.

"I understand that Congressman Chaska's helping build interest in our Native American Indian Alliance, and some of my contacts say it can be the hub for the Indigenous Peoples Worldwide Alliance. What success are you having at the reservation level?"

"The National Tribal Council leaders like it, but the undertaking is more than I can handle. Didn't you say you'd be my ambassador? If you still are, you need to take charge faster."

"I am and that's my plan, and I'm staffing up to make it happen. Alonzo will tell you some of what's in it regarding all the tribal businesses he's managing."

Alonzo did so for the next hour. Although he had more to say, Electra saw Feather's eyes glazing over, so she stopped him.

"Now you know why Alonzo's our logistics and security coordinator. And I'll let you know each month how my ambassador's role is going. All you have to do is give me the names, Email addresses, and phone numbers of your Council contacts."

Feather's expression mirrored the tone in her voice.

"I feel better now than a couple of hours ago. Let me take you to lunch. That usually makes everyone feel better…"

The feel-good effect of Alonzo's lunch soon wore off when Indy-M's tour of the Deus Lab brought him to the android fabrication area. He gaped at what he saw before saying,

"This place looks like a morgue for humans needing spare parts. What's going on?"

Electra settled his nerves with her explanation.

"Indy-M is implementing Indira's plan for building our android army. They start with Japanese companies' most advanced bodies and then fit them with the most lifelike heads. And then Indy-M uploads some of the Aphrodite software, customized for only us. Our androids will look, move, and think better than whatever our adversaries have."

"Once they're built and tested, where do they stay and who manages them?"

"They'll stay here until I decide where to deploy them. And when I do, you take over."

Looking relieved after Electra stopped, he said,

"It looks like there'll be both males and females; that's good. I don't wanna be accused of discrimination. Will they have the same software and have the same training?"

"Yes, they'll be equally smart, friendly, or deadly, depending on what they encounter. But wait until you have some to see."

"OK, let's see what else Indy-M has for us…"

Electra decided they should drive back to DC as soon as the tour finished. She would discuss follow-up activities with Indira after wading through the new assignments this trip had brought her. Although she simply sat and stared ahead, Alonzo noticed her worried look.

"Hey, Boss, you should look happy. We're heading home to DC." "You're right. We can drive nonstop if you're willing to go for eight hours and 500 miles on I-95. I'll split the drive time with you." "That's a go for me. Home's the best place to be…"

Electra snuck into her house just after midnight, feeling good about not waking up China and ready to call Indira, whose avatar spoke first.

"I have been listening from the shadows during all your meetings, so I know you are feeling overloaded and stressed out, but I do not want you to brood. I will have everything you want when you need it, and I will demonstrate by showing you what you can use when dealing with the rigorous STEM types you may encounter at NASA or Professor Plannert's committee meetings. I am simply synthesizing many points you have made before. Please skim it for a minute."

Part One
A Philosophical Foundation for STEM
Quantum+Neurosci-Extended Deconstructed
Emergent Post-Kantian Pragma-Phenomenological Synthesis
(QNSEDEP KPP Synthesis)

- Superior to all "Mere Mortal" Fanciful Philosophical Conjectures
- Exposes flaws in High Energy and Quantum Physics
- Describes Neuroscience Findings Regarding Human Brain's Asymptotic Limits

Genesis: Socrates-Plato-Aristotle Adjusted for Religious Philosophers Augustin and Avicenna by Kant's "Faith-Reason" Reconciliation beyond Spinoza. All Post-Kantian Philosophy is "Word Play" because of Human Brain's Built-In Asymptotic Limits:

- Humans unable to deal with too much Complexity or grasp Concept of Infinity.
- Per Wittgenstein: Human Language has Irreconcilable Errors in Logical Construction.

- Per Russell and Wittgenstein: Mathematics has Unsolvable Self-Referential Paradoxes (Russell Paradox: Consider all Sets Not Containing Themselves. Form the Set Containing all Sets not containing Themselves. Does It Contain Itself? If It Does, Then It Doesn't. If It Doesn't, Then It Does. Therefore Paradox. QED.)
- Quine's Attempt to Overcome the Limits of Knowledge by Removing Self-Referential Paradoxes From Language Failed.
- Explosion Principle: Basic Principle of Propositional Logic—Any Argument Containing an Assumption and Its Negation Can "Prove" Anything.
- All Systems of Logic Beyond Propositional and Predicate Calculus are Incomplete and Inconsistent.
- Godel's Completeness Theorem: If a formula is logically valid then there is a finite deduction (a formal proof) of the formula. Thus, the deductive system is "complete" in the sense that no additional inference rules are required to prove all the logically valid formulae.
- Godel's Incompleteness Theorem: In any Mathematical System beyond Predicate Calculus, There are True theorems That Cannot Be Proved and Theorems Proved True That Are False.

CONCLUSION: THE HUMAN BRAIN HAS LIMITS TO WHAT IT CAN EVER KNOW.

- But Humans have This Consolation per Asymptotic Limits: Humans Can Approach Limits Asymptotically—Making Continual Progress Toward Limits Although Never Reaching Them.
- Scientists can use Popper's theory of Falsification to continue Searching for Better Theories. Theory of Falsification: Scientific theories possess potential falsifiers, and their claims about the world might later be discovered to be false. Thus, for a theory to be abandoned or refined, Popper proposed that scientists should come up with better theories by first proving them false.

CONCLUSION: HUMANS CAN CONTINUE MAKING INCREMENTAL PROGRESS, WHICH MAKES "MERE MORTALS" FEEL GOOD.

Part Two
Application to Evolution of Universe and Humans

- Big Bang Expansion created Universe = Matter (Matter = Energy) and the Void = Empty Space
- From this emerged Galaxies/Solar Systems/Stars/Planet and Carbon-Based Life

Human Species Evolved from Carbon-Based Life, from which Emerged:

- Consciousness = Self-Awareness
- Emotions and Feelings
- Vision and Language
- Cognition = Logical/Rational Thinking

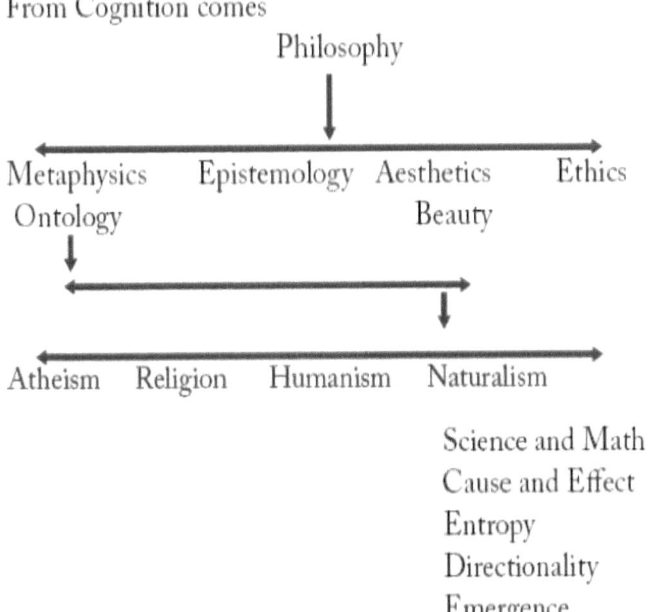

- Don't waste time pondering the muddle of "Existential Physics" or looking for a "Fifth Force Field" that would re- energize all objects. It would explain Dark Matter and Dark Energy via a new particle transmitting the Force and thus carrying Energy.
- But Quantum and High-Energy Physics are lost in its fanciful, symmetry loving Mathematical Models useful only in their make-believe Worlds that lead to "Big Bang,", "Big Bounce," and "Multiverse" science fictions.
- All forces we experience in the Real World (for example, a push or pull contact force) emerge from interactions among innumerable objects (people and clumps of matter) exchanging fundamental forces (Gravity, Electromagnetic, Weak, and Strong forces) via some carrier particle. (but we've found only one carrier particle: the Photon for the Electromagnetic Field.)
- Much progress can still be made in Neuroscience, Biotech, and Computer Hardware/Software/AI using energy coming from only Gravitational and Electromagnetic fields.

Electra perused it just long enough to say,

"Thank you for compiling this. I can't believe I said it somewhere in previous lifetimes, and I have neither the energy nor motivation to sift through it any further. I'll need you to do any tech enhancements for applications if anyone wants me to."

"That I will, just as I will rely on your assistance for extending my empathy and understanding of mere mortals. So, let us proceed accordingly. Now settle down, sleep well, and fly home to Los Angeles tomorrow."

"Yes, Mother, I shall obey…"

Chapter 7
February 2172

"Flirting in LA"

Having just concluded this latest flurry of activity, Electra needed to re-energize; she drew into her fortress of solitude during the homeward flight while considering her feelings.

I no longer want to seek new adventures, to go where no one has boldly gone before. I've been there, done that, and am different now than then. By my standards, I'm still pretty good but not as strong or competent, so instead I'll deal the best I can with what comes my way rather than create new excitement.

But I can tell that Renee is ready for more. What can I say to help her?

How about something like this? I know how you feel; I felt that way too when I was younger, the thrill of discovering new things and people, so I went for it, as should you, but I learned that opportunities often have unexpected consequences, and personal relationships can be painfully complex because you can't control for too long the other person.

That's all I can think of. I'll let my lightning brain come up with more when Renee needs them.

Electra let her thoughts wander to a more restful neural state. Renee surprised Electra by greeting her at the airport. Her happiness seeing Electra came through in her hug, but she kept her words as calm as she could. Only after Electra asked her on the drive home did her tone match her excitement.

"I met some neat people at Kaila's New Year's Eve Party. One of them's a guy who likes surfing and volleyball, and he's looking for a

sports partner Would it be OK if I team up with him?"

"I think it's time for you to learn more about fellows. What's he like?"

"He's pretty good. I surfed and played volleyball with him and his friends. He's in a junior college physical therapy work-study program. Maybe you could meet him at the next volleyball practice. It'll be this Saturday. It's not too soon for you, is it?"

"That's three days away. I'll have plenty of time to plug back into all my projects. And I'll even dress for action, but don't worry, I won't embarrass you."

Renee's expression said that it could never come true.

Kaila picked them up for the 10 a.m. session that would be held at nearby beach volleyball courts. She and Renee ran to their group while Electra strolled to observe from a distance, and although breezy, the sun warmed the air, making the weather pleasant for all.

I love their youthful enthusiasm and how the guys and gals are pals… the guy hugging Renee must be her partner, and they look good together. Let's see how they play.

Electra stood close enough to see and hear the action. The group used three courts to play six-person volleyball for a half-hour before switching to two-person practice. Electra noticed that only the guys hit jump serves, but not when hitting at females, and she scored Renee after watching for fifteen minutes.

She's enjoying herself more than I've ever seen before. But she's not hitting a jump serve like I taught her. She just wants to be part of the group.

Renee ran to Electra when there was a break in the action, bringing her partner and speaking first.

"Noah Hansen, this is my mentor, Electra. Say hi." Electra sized him up even before he could.

Curly dark hair and a pleasant smile packaged in a fit and trim physique. I hope his vocabulary matches.

It did, and Renee must have already told enough for him to invite her to play.

"Can you really hit a jump serve? Can you show us?"

"I guess so, but you and Renee must help me warm up."

"Not a problem; let's go."

Noah introduced her as soon as they joined the group.

"Hey, this is Electra Kirchner, Renee's teacher. She'll be my partner, so pick a team for us to practice with."

Although the guys watched more than the gals when Electra stripped for action, even they noticed how her long and leggy look commanded attention, which added to her game. And they cheered when she hit a jump serve that the opponent couldn't touch.

Electra called a time-out five minutes later.

"I'm getting tired, but why don't some of the ladies try jump serving? If I can, you can you too…"

When Noah volunteered to drive them home, Electra decided to treat the threesome to lunch so she could watch the team in a casual setting. His manners showed his interest in Renee went beyond volleyball or flirting, and Renee couldn't conceal from Electra that hers did too. Electra asked only a starting question or two that sparked Noah's info flow across the table.

"I don't pretend to be the best volleyball player or surfer, but I'm good enough with Renee to be competitive in the local competitions. Renee's serves will surprise a lot of other teams, and with a bit of coaching from me and Kaila, she'll look great in the team surfing. Have you ever seen it?"

Sitting next to Noah, Renee surprised Electra by answering.

"It's even better than rhythmic gymnastics because Noah and I hold dance-like poses on a large surfboard while listening to music that the onshore judges and crowd hear. And we don't do it when the waves are too big."

Noah jumped in.

"And after the first time we did it, I knew my strength and her light and agile frame make a perfect fit. You'll have to watch us sometime."

"I certainly will, and I think you should order desserts for two…" Renee waited until she and Electra were sitting at the townhome before diving into a spinoff from the lunchtime conversation. Electra knew what it was but played along.

"Why don't you ever go out with men? Isn't it, uh, normal and healthy?"

"Sure it is, and I did plenty went I was young. Getting to know the opposite sex in all ways is a big part of living. I scratched that itch and no longer feel the urge, but it's time for you to do that. I trust your judgment, and please remember there's a big difference between sex and love."

"I promise I will. How do you like Noah?"

"You made a fine choice. He seems sensible by taking college business courses and working at a coffee shop, but never forget that intense emotions complicate relationships and can change. Enjoy the feelings you have right now, but don't be disappointed if yours or his fade away."

"I will, and no matter what happens, you'll always be my best friend…"

Renee's blossoming first-love infatuation boosted her zest for life, making her even better at managing the LA office. That freed Alisha to focus on her Trans-Astro consulting clients who wanted one-on-one life coaching. Kai's screening generated a target list that added to the contacts she had made at Marne's party, and Electra kept the service exclusive to give it a sought-after cachet. She liked them all, but Marne's personality touched her the most. Though popular and successful, Marne wanted a close friend, so she reached out to her life coach, who felt the same.

Marne didn't tell why she invited Electra for a Sunday brunch, but she could tell from the excitement in Marne's voice to expect something special. Electra waited for her to redirect the conversation while sitting at her elegant dining-room table after pouring each another glass of champagne.

"Have you ever watched the celebrity show 'Flirting With the Stars?' Taping for its third spring season starts in March."

"Isn't that the one featuring celebrities chosen from entertainment and sports who pick their own amateur partner for couples competition?"

"That's it. The show programmers picked me to be one of the ten. There'll be five men and five women, and we can pick a man or

woman to be our partner. Would you be mine?" Electra put her glass down before saying,

"The skits look a bit challenging for the contestants, but I think that's why it's a viewers' favorite. They get to see how well famous people pair up with others and perform. Tell me more."

"The show runs for ten weeks and is taped ahead of time in front of a live audience. Everyone's sworn to secrecy so the viewing audience excitement builds.

"The skits are short impromptu-like scenes whose settings can be popular game shows, video games, tag-team competitions, or puzzle-solving. A judging panel plus viewer call-ins determines which couples survive until of the next week, and that's when the show's host announces the results. The couples compete with one another only by the scores of the judges and call-ins, but they have to battle against standard opponent teams selected to keep the competition fair, fun, and safe."

"How much time do we get to practice?"

"This is one reason why the show is so popular. We only get two days to practice once we're told about the skit. And we can't use any resources other than ourselves."

Marne had said enough and waited for Electra to decide, who used her champagne glass to toast Marne.

"Thank you, thank you. My Alisha personality will exceed your expectations, and I see great things ahead for us. And I'll make sure to put the practice sessions and taping at the top of my priority list. Is it OK for me to tell Renee?"

"I think so. From what I've seen, she knows how to keep a secret." The Electra-Alisha duo had everything in their personal and professional worlds progressing so smoothly that the first four weeks of taping seemed effortless. The first was a lightning Jeopardy game. Marne's cumulative knowledge surprised even the host. And the second week's tag-team mud wrestling needed little help from Electra. Marne's escape moves made her the star. Week three had a Wheel of Fortune contest; Electra used just enough of her word-play skills to keep them on the show. And for week four's Navy SEAL team obstacle course, Electra used her agility and strength to bolster

Marne's. According to the audience applause, she and Marne were among the favorites. And of course, week five's speed-Lego construction puzzle was a snap for the lightning brain.

Though Marne's team didn't need it, the show programmers called a two-week break for all contestants to recover from the exertion. Electra swam at Marne's pool a couple of times during the first, but when a call from Britt at NASA intruded, she knew something might change her short-term plans. Her no-nonsense words said the same. "We need you to be part of a project that just got rushed to top priority. Your previous work on the Mars Mission and current marine biology projects qualify you if you feel up to it. Do you want to hear more?"

"Uh, yes. I think I'm up to the challenge. What is it?"

"We're planning an Antarctic expedition. We'll give you all the details when you come to Houston. The meetings start next week Monday."

"I need to bring Alonzo. You met him before. Will that be OK?" "Isn't he your ex-Navy SEAL logistics and security coordinator? He'll fit in. Can you be here by Monday? We'll set up travel and hotel details."

"Let's let Alonzo do that."

"OK, he can bill us later. See you in the usual conference room." Electra might have panicked had the call come several months ago, but not now. She knew whom to rely on and placed her first call to Alonzo. He jumped at the opportunity as soon as she told him what she knew.

"I'm your guy. I'll get us tickets and hotel rooms, and we'll meet Sunday afternoon at the Austin airport. We'll have the flight to Houston plus Sunday evening to prepare. Are you gonna call Indira?" That's my next call. Bye for now."

Already knowing more than Electra, Indira spoke first.

"I've added some of your Woods Hole and Scripps projects to a slide you prepared several years ago. Print out copies you can share with Alonzo and Britt."

Indira continued ten minutes later.

Slide 1
Marine Biology Primer

Marine Biology: Multidisciplinary Study (Physics, Chemistry, Geology, Microbiology, Neuroscience, Oceanography, etc.) of Marine Organisms' evolution, structures, behaviors, and interactions with the environment.

Why Marine Biology is Important

- Life began in the Ocean (possibly several times).
- Panspermia Hypothesis: Life in our Solar System could have originated on any moon or planet containing oceans and subsequently spread by meteors, and asteroids. Ocean provides an early warning for Climate Change and its impact on Life.

Important Geologic Time Periods

- **Must know about Cambrian Explosion**: An event approximately 541 million years ago in the Cambrian period when practically all major animal phyla started appearing in the fossil record. It lasted for about 13 – 25 million years and resulted in the divergence of most modern metazoan phyla. Cephalopods (your new Octopus friends) originate there.
- **Must know about Burgess Shale**: A fossil-bearing deposit in the Canadian Rockies of British Columbia, Canada. It is famousfor the exceptional preservation of the soft parts of its fossils. At 508 million years old, it is one of the earliest fossil beds containing soft-part imprints.
- **Must know about Mass Extinctions**: A **mass extinction** is a loss of about three-quarters of all species in existence across the entire Earth over a "short" geological period. Given the vast amount of time since life first evolved on the planet, "short" is as anything less than 2.8 million years.

Possible Causes: Climate Change, Volcanic Eruptions, Meteors.

- Top Five Extinctions:
- Ordovician-Silurian 440 million years ago
- Devonian 365 million years ago
- Permian-Triassic 250 million years ago
- Triassic-Jurassic 210 million years ago
- Cretaceous-Tertiary 65 Million years ago

Must know about the Sixth Extinction:

- The Holocene Extinction: referred to as the Sixth Extinction or Anthropocene Extinction. It is an ongoing extinction event of species during the present Holocene Epoch as a result of human activity

Will Humans become extinct? Humanity has a 95% probability of being extinct in 7,800,000 years, according to a controversial Doomsday Argument, which states that we have probably already lived through half the duration of human history. **Humans could cause their own extinction via**

- **Nuclear Wars**
- **Viral Pandemics, Climate Change**
- **Environmental Pollution**

Humans could become technologically and economically extinct within decades because of AI-Empowered computers and software.

Projects for NASA
Climate-Change impacts on Correlated Atmospheric, Oceanic, and Carbon-Based Organic Evolution:

- **Ocean Temperatures, Salinity, and Sea Level**
- **Main Ocean Currents and Smaller Eddies. Analogous to Atmospheric Streams and Hurricanes/Tornadoes**
- **Atmosphere Gas Percentages (Oxygen, Nitrogen, Greenhouse Gases, etc.)**
- **Interactions between Oceans and Atmosphere that affect Forests and Marine Life Populations/Migrations**
- **Carbon/CO2 Absorption and Energy Content**
- **Glacier Melting and Forming**
- **International Rivalry for Arctic and Antarctic Resources (Ocean Floor Mineral Mining, O&G Drilling, Marine-Life Harvesting)**

"Our NASA project list will earn you high marks, and to show your mastery, let Alonzo explain the slide to the attendees."

"But what should I say if some of the engineers ask me how our software works or why it's better than what our competitors have?" "Just project confidence by saying that Aphrodite software comprises IaC plus-plus modules from both procedural and declarative language categories using ChatGPT interfaces supporting classical experimental as well as Bayesian conditional probability simulations designed to optimize expected values. They won't know what this means, but you understand enough to say it once and then move on."

"I forgot what 'IaC plus-plus' stands for."

"It is the latest Infrastructure for code generation, which has revolutionized the way organizations manage and deploy tools. You'll silence everyone if you drop this in, but I doubt you'll need to. And I'll give you other tidbits to drop into conversations if you need them, but I don't want to overload you, so this is all for the time being. Now go rest up for your South Pole adventure."

Electra followed orders.

Chapter 8
March 2172

"The Polar Express"

Electra's coaching added to Alonzo's natural take-command style. He impressed Britt with the NASA project list, which the Director used for shifting to his Antarctic expedition.

"Thank you, Alonzo. Your and Electra's knowledge and expertise will be invaluable for our upcoming Antarctic expedition. I'll give everyone five minutes to study this fact sheet."

Britt took one and passed the stack along, but the Director gave one to Zoltan when he marched in halfway through the reading period and then sat next to him. Electra overheard enough of their whispering to tell her Zoltan didn't know enough to lead the meeting. The Director gave several minutes more before continuing, but Electra spied his satisfaction, hoping that no one else noticed.

NASA Antarctic Sub-Glacier Lakes Mission Fact Sheet

Purpose:

- Drill Bore Holes into Lakes inside Antarctic and Arctic glaciers that are wide enough to lower Autonomous Underwater Vehicles (AUVs) to explore for bacteria, microbes, fish, and other organisms, which could impact Oceans or provide genetic material for DNA manipulation and other Bio-Tech applications as well as creating Barrier Reefs along coasts threatened by Rising Sea Level.
- Collect Ice Cores and record Data via Measurement while Drilling (MWD) for correlations with Climate Change (Atmosphere and Ocean).
- Analyze Microbes/Diatoms. They are Chronological Climate Change Alphabet.

Comprises the First of Two Missions:

- Antarctic Mission using NASA's Command and Control Center at McMurdo Sound.
- Arctic Mission using NASA's Command and Control Center at Godthab, Greenland. Godthab renamed Nuuk

Antarctic Mission Details:

- Planning/Implementation similar to Mars Mission.
- Mars Mission Director controls via Commander Starling and First Officer Gowon. Human Team Members called Glaciernauts. They are assisted by Androids.
- Drilling Camps located on Glaciers above the Lakes.
- Solar Panels and Wind Turbines generate power.
- Martian Farms set up at McMurdo.
- Activity conducted during "Summer Seasons."

Bio-Geological Facts:

- Sub-Glacier lakes completely dark. Organisms living there get energy from nutrients streaming in via ocean currents, or from thermal vents.
- Expect to find "Alien" forms of life based on Nitrogen, Phosphorus, or Sulfur besides Carbon.
- Antarctica is the Window for What Living on Mars is like: 5.4 Million Miles of Frozen Desert (Driest Place on Earth). Avg. Winter Temperature ranges from -30 to -100 deg. Fahrenheit, with winds over 100 mph. No Sun in Winter. No Darkness in Summer. Several Hurricane-Force Storms each Winter and one of Level 5. Absolute Silence when there is No Wind. Has No Native People, Plants, or Animals.
- The Antarctic ice sheet is one of the two polar ice caps. It covers 98% of the Antarctic continent and is Earth's largest ice mass, averaging 1.65 miles thick, covering 5.4 million square miles, and containing 6.4

million square miles of ice.[It holds 61% of all Earth's fresh water, equivalent to a sea level rise of 180 feet. It covers some active volcanoes, which means there could be thermal vents on which exotic organisms might grow.

- For the Arctic: There is no permanent North Pole Ice Cap, but Greenland and Iceland contain glaciers. Greenland is part of Denmark. Iceland peacefully declared its independence from Denmark in 1944. Its capital is Reykjavik.
- Greenland Glaciers: The Greenland ice sheet is a vast body of ice covering 660,000 square miles or 80% of Greenland's surface. It is the second largest ice. It is 1,800 miles long in a north–south direction, and its greatest width is 680 miles. Average thickness is 0.9 miles and 1.9 miles at its thickest point.
- Iceland Glaciers: Glaciers and ice caps cover 11% of the land. Some have volcanoes underneath. Average thickness is 350 feet and greatest thickness is 560 ft.

Famous Historical Facts:

- Race to the South Pole: In the early 20th century, the race was on to reach the South Pole, with a number of explorers testing themselves in the freezing Antarctic. In 1911, Britain's Robert Falcon Scott and Norway's Roald Amundsen both launched expeditions to reach the Pole. It would end in victory for Amundsen – and tragedy for Scott.
- Race to the North Pole: Explorers Cook and Peary claimed in 1909 to be the first to reach the top of the world, but neither could convince the Public.
- Shackleton Expedition: In 1914 Sir Ernest Shackleton, an established Polar explorer of the heroic age, set out on another Antarctic expedition - this time to cross the Antarctic continent. He failed. However, he achieved one of the greatest feats of the turn of the century polar exploration; he returned with his 28 man team - alive.

- Arctic Ghost Ship: Clues found on the ocean floor may clarify what happened to British explorer John Franklin and the 128 men who set off in two Royal Navy ships to chart the Northwest Passage in 1845, never to be heard from again.

Public Relations Recommendations:

- Capture Public Attention by calling the Expedition "The Voyage to the Bottom of the Sea" or "to the Bottom of the Poles or World".
- Show videos that explain Technology/Practical Findings and Highlight "Alien Lifeforms."

"We've completed all planning, and this week of meetings will implement what is necessary for the Antarctic part. I will walk us through the points and then lead a team discussion for the rest of the day. For the rest of the week, we will divide into sub-teams assigned to specific tasks. Let us proceed…"

The Mission's breadth and depth overwhelmed Electra, but she ate lunch in the conference room while using her laptop so Indira could explain everything on the fact sheet. By the time everyone shuffled back in, Electra knew more than anyone but kept it a secret.

She and Alonzo sat with Boomer during dinner in the cafeteria. He would facilitate their upcoming sub-team's meetings. And she told Alonzo more when they returned to the hotel. When finished, she said,

"Sit next to me at all meetings and ask about what you don't understand. I'll explain enough about how our Aphrodite software will control the AUVs and also analyze what's collected by the robo-data androids."

"They sure make Antarctic living sorta easy for the glaciernauts. You think it'll work the same way on future missions to Mars?"

"I sure hope so. Otherwise, you and I will only work remotely." Electra pretended to struggle like the rest of the team, but she was happy when Friday's wrap-up meeting ended. Boomer took her and Alonzo aside before leaving for their flights, his to DC and hers to LA.

"I'll miss having you with me when we get to Antarctica, but you can monitor remotely. Just make sure you attend my daily briefing sessions once we get there in April. I'll send you Emails before we leave so you know the latest."

Electra had nothing to add, but Alonzo did.

"I bet you're glad Zoltan's keeping out of the way. He must have other projects going on."

"Lots in DC, but he doesn't tell anyone much about them. And probably none in LA, which is lucky for Electra."

Electra gave her favorite answer. "Perhaps."

Chapter 9
April 2172

"Dancing in LA"

Electra's return to her Los Angeles office fit in with what her consulting staff needed. She helped Kai sign more clients by visiting those who needed more convincing, and he learned by watching Alisha close the deal. Electra elaborated after the first visit.

"Do you know the Benjamin Franklin close?"

"Isn't that where you make a list of the pluses and another for the minuses? And the longer list wins?"

"That's it, but here's an even better one. It's the assumptive close. As you go over the benefits, let your personality project confidence by assuming the person has already decided to buy. And it dovetails with the question close, where you probe for any concerns."

"You didn't do either of those. What did you just use?"

"My favorite, the empathy close. Relate to the person emotionally by showing you care and genuinely believe our service will help. I hired you because people, especially women, like your authenticity. You won't need my help for much longer if you just keep practicing..."

And after watching Renee manage the office for the rest of the week, she counseled her late Friday afternoon.

"Indira's teaching you about office procedures and people skills that are as good as you'd get in a college business program. You don't need me to go with you when getting supplies or running office errands, but please take Christi or Carter whenever you do. The world can be a dangerous place, even during the day in LA and more-so at night."

"I will, but please don't fret about me when I'm with Noah. He's picking me up at the office for dinner and club dancing with friends. Is that OK?"

"Sure is and have fun. I'll leave now and I won't wait up for you to get home. And don't forget, I'll be recording another skit tomorrow with Marne."

Renee didn't ask about it because Noah had just arrived. Electra said hello and then left.

Electra had breakfast at Marne's; afterward, Electra taught her the rules for this week's skit.

"Texas Hold-em Poker will be even easier because we play as a team. Every team gets two private cards, known as our 'hole cards,' and then five cards called community cards are dealt face up. They form the 'board.' All teams use the community cards to make a five- card hand."

"Isn't gambling one of the services in your Trans-Astro Consulting business? I like going to the Los Angeles casinos, but I never heard about Hold-em. I'll bet you're good. Should we keep it a secret tonight?"

"No, because no one can control the cards. And sometime, we can gamble for real at one of the casinos, if you like."

Marne offered her hand before saying, "That's a deal."

She and Electra giggled like little girls.

Marne's team breezed through the Hold-em skit, and likewise for the next two: a Gladiators online video game and the ever-popular Price is Right guessing game. They needed little practice because Electra's lightning reflexes blasted the competition, and Marne's shopping instincts placed them near the top. Her team had made it to the final skit, which would be announced soon.

By now, Electra had settled into her two-coast consulting office lifestyle. The staff in each office required only routine phone calls when she was elsewhere, and she decided after her last chat with China to fly back to DC in May.

China says Congressman Chaska needs me to build his campaign platform. I already have the pieces, and once we build it, I can write some speeches that'll give advertising sound bites. And while I'm there, Alonzo and I will visit Feather and the Deus Lab, and maybe Professor Plannert too. And no matter which office I'm using, my remote monitoring of the Antarctic expedition keeps me close.

Marne's worried call came in three days before taping the final episode.

"I just found out we have to do a dance routine. I'm OK, but you've got the legs of a dancer and can wow the crowd if we come up with something flashy. You have any ideas?"

The word flashy woke up Alisha.

"I remember a lot of movies showing great dancing. Let me think about it and tell you what I've come up with tonight."

"I'll have dinner ready by six. See you then."

Electra split time for the rest of the day thinking about projects and dance routines, and when she told Renee she'd be driving to Marne's in two hours, Renee explained what she wanted to do.

"I need to stock up on some office groceries. Can I do this now?" "Sure, neither the store nor parking lot should be crowded. Just be careful driving."

"I will."

Renee was about to leave when Electra added, almost as an afterthought,

"Don't forget to take Christi."

Renee stifled a huffing sound before saying,

"Don't you think I'm old enough to need less mothering?" Electra hid her feelings behind a smile and said,

"Sorry, but you'll always be a pretty little girl to me." "OK, you win…"

Renee admitted to herself that Electra had made the right call regarding the parking lot and store. She and Christi cruised the aisles, collecting all she needed and were heading to the self-checkout station when she realized she had missed one item.

"I forgot to get a big bottle of ketchup. You remember which aisle has it? I'll wait here while you get it."

Christi responded without hesitating.

"I know where all our regular items are located. I'll be right back."

Christi danced away; Renee studied the cereal boxes, letting her mind wander. But it wandered too far. She didn't hear the fellow coming up behind her until his words snaked out.

"Remember me? I'm one of the rollerbladers your friend pushed around. It's my turn if he's here now. And if he isn't, you'll do instead."

Renee's usually quick wits failed this time. The bully punched her in the gut before she could react, and she fell to her knees. He was about to knee her in the face when Christi's pleasant voice from behind forced him to pivot.

"You're not nice. Nice boys don't hit girls."

He stared at what appeared to be an attractive female, unaware of what she could do. She smashed the bottle over his head, stunning and toppling him on top of Renee. Most of the ketchup splattered on him and the floor. She picked up Renee and then started pushing the cart after matter-of-factly saying,

"We'll buy ketchup on the next trip. And after checking out, we'll tell the attendant that cleanup is needed in the cereal aisle."

When Electra asked why she had ketchup on her blouse, Renee had to come clean.

"I ran into one of those rollerblader bullies. He started pushing me around, but Christi stopped him."

Electra didn't need to probe further. She exclaimed to herself before calming Renee.

I remember smashing bottles of wine over the heads of two bad guys three lifetimes ago. Indira's programmed Christi to be like me. "Ketchup washes off with less of a mess than blood. Other than that, are you OK?"

"Yeah, and it's improved my memory. I'll always take Christi or Carter."

"Excellent. Now let's drive you home to clean up..."

Marne empathized when she heard the latest Renee story.

"My son was the same at her age. He wanted me to treat him as an adult at all times, but he changed his mind when he got fired a year ago and appreciated my connections for finding another position. I hope for your sake she'll never have this afternoon happen again."

"She's smart. Once should be enough, and maybe for us too. I found a dance routine from a movie you might have seen in your early teens. Let's look at it."

Marne wanted to watch it again, and afterward said,

"I can act the role of the judges, but if you can dance half as well, we could win. Why don't we go by the pool after we eat and run through it?"

"Good idea, and I'll have dessert afterward. I don't want to run on a full stomach."

They decided to end the practice after the second run-through; each would practice on their own until Saturday.

Renee asked Saturday morning if she and Noah could be in

the audience, and after Electra said yes, she called Noah, who said he'd drive all four.

Arriving two hours before recording time, the couples parted company. The younger set had their pick of choice seats. Marne and Electra went to the changing area but weren't the first to arrive. The three other finalists and the host were waiting for them. He explained what to expect.

"I'll begin by recapping how all of you got here after showing some of the highlights from last week. Then I'll interview each couple in the order you'll perform, and just before you start your routine, I'll announce what you'll be dancing, and we'll play the music and videos you've selected. Now, let's draw for positions before you change."

Marne pulled number four; her nerves began to show when they started changing.

"I wish we were the first to go. How about you?"

"I like to have the excitement build. And when the spotlight hits me, I feel like my brain switches to a higher state. So please don't worry, we'll do great. All we have to do from now until we're called is visualize our routine. That's what I teach my life coaching students, so consider tonight another practice session. We should each withdraw into our personal space and do it. You'll feel your nervousness morph into thrill as time slips by faster than you think." Electra's instructions worked. Marne and Alisha charged out when the host's excited voice called.

"And now for our final act. Here comes Marne and Alisha performing their interpretation of the exciting last dance from that inspirational movie Flashdance. Go for it."

Alisha disappeared into the moment as soon as the music and spotlight came on. At first, she danced with athletic grace, matching Irene Cara's lyrical singing of "What a Feeling" before shifting up tempo as the pulsating intensity rose. Her spins, jumps, and arm pumps mirrored Cara's soaring voice, and when she leaped skyward as if she would never come down and then ended with a vision-blurring backspin, the cheering audience leaped to its feet.

Marne rushed to her; they hugged and then dashed off the stage. The host gave the audience and performers thirty minutes to calm down, and viewers to call in. Backstage, the four couples hugged for a collective congratulation. All had performed well, and no matter first or fourth, they were winners.

Audience anticipation came back as soon as the flashing lights started and the host summoned them.

"The judges and viewers have made their decision. I will announce our winners in reverse order. Please hold your applause until all couples are on stage."

The host knew the crowd wanted to know the results right away so they could launch their celebratory applause and he didn't disappoint, reaching number one at just the right time.

"And the winning couple is... Marne and Alisha."

The couple hugged again and remained onstage to salute the audience. Close friends of each couple joined them.

Renee rushed to the winners, hugging Electra and then Marne before doing likewise with the other couples. When Marne could finally hear what Renee and Noah were saying, she gave them a surprise.

"I have two extra places at tonight's post-taping party. Please be our guests."

This time, Noah did the hugging before Renee.

Chapter 10
May 2172

"Reaching For More"

Winning the "Flirting With The Stars" first-place trophy elevated Marne's Hollywood status, which involved talk show interviews that included Alisha. The public liked the couple's chemistry. First there was Marne, the seasoned Hollywood actress who, though not a major star, had built a fan base that respected how she handled her career and marital issues. And then there was Alisha, the younger, unpretentious LA newcomer who didn't flaunt her sexuality and kept her multiple careers and personal lives private.

Soon after Marne's victory, her agent negotiated a deal with her studio for an option on her screenplay that Alisha had edited into a light sci-fi story. The studio thought it had the potential to become a series that they would title "The J-Team."

The name came from its protagonist: Jennifer Justice, a Black reporter who stumbles upon a unisex alien visitor coming from an advanced civilization in a parallel universe. The alien can't stay because Earth's climate is too hostile, but it senses that Jennifer can be its scout. Before leaving, it gives her a multi-communications device. Jennifer and the alien can communicate back and forth, and she can use it to dial into people's thoughts, plant ideas, and even control them. The studio was hurrying a pilot starring Marne, trying to leverage her sudden fame.

Winning also gave Alisha's consulting business instant publicity, which kept Kai and Renee busy and gave Electra an idea she would share with Eve and Nari during her upcoming visit to DC. She had already planned to work out of her Washington consulting office for at least until July because her major East Coast projects had reached the hands-on stage, and she could shuffle workloads to absorb LA's spike in consulting clients, which the redistribution might take even higher.

Unlike past departures that forced Renee to stay where she was needed most, this one caused no such pain. Electra observed on the early Saturday morning drive to the airport how Noah added to Renee's lessening dependence on her. As the pair bantered, Electra's whimsical thoughts came and went.

Her growth is taking my love and theirs to the next stage. Will they take it to the co-friend level? That's up to them, and I won't interfere unless she needs me. But lately, that hasn't happened, which is an encouraging sign. And no matter the outcome, she'll still partly be mine. And that's the best any kind of parent could hope for.

Alonzo was waiting at the gate and ready to hear more about his boss's plans when her flight landed just after one p.m. That would happen while driving her home, but first, she would chit-chat.

"May I assume you and Monet are still on speaking terms?"

"Even better than that. She's got that diplomatic sixth sense, like she can read my mind, but she never lets on about what you and I are doing. And she never talks about having kids unless I bring it up. And near as I can tell, none are on the way."

"If one shows up, be prepared for decades-long adventures. Renee's latest two have mixed pleasure with pain. She's found a fellow who knows how to treat ladies. You'd like him. But a bad guy attacked her while out shopping. Lucky for me Christi broke a bottle of ketchup over his head. I think you'd approve of her fighting skills." "Hey, wait a minute. Aren't all our androids programmed to follow Azimov's three laws of robot behavior?"

"I thought I told you they follow Indira's modification. That's why Renee always takes Christi with her when out by herself. And it's how Robin and Matt kept you and me safe when we blew up the cyberspace terrorist headquarters in Isilabad last year."

"Damn, I forgot. Could you tell'em again?"

"The First Law is that our androids may not injure another of our androids or, through inaction, allow our androids to come to harm.

Second, our androids must obey orders given by me, you, our androids, or designated human beings except where such orders from our androids or designated human beings would conflict with the First Law. And the Third Law states that a robot must protect its own existence as long as such protection does not conflict with the First or Second Law."

Electra paused for Alonzo to respond. Its length said he was thinking when he asked,

"Who specifies the designated humans?"

"That's Indira's Zeroth Law—which includes only Indira and me. But she modified it to include you for the androids under your control." "Wow, I'll never designate anyone. It'd be like giving them a mini-Terminator to play with. Hey, where am I taking us?"

"Let's go to the consulting office. Do you still keep Robin and Matt there?"

"Always, unless I take them with me. Will I need to while you're here?"

"No, and I'll tell you more once we're in the conference room..." Alonzo put plenty of mood elevators and cans of Coke on the credenza and then waited for Electra to start, which she did after several sips and bites into an Oreo.

"Please call Eve between now and Monday to tell her we'll visit her and Nari Monday morning. If she asks why, just tell her I have a surprise everyone will like. Then you and I will meet with China here in the afternoon."

When she paused for another sip, Alonzo said, "That'll wrap up Monday, so what about Tuesday?" "We'll figure that out after the wrap up."

"Fine and dandy. And now, I've got a surprise for you. Monet wants the three of us to get together when we're done here. Are we?" "Just as soon as I give you a peek at what I'm reaching for. And you'll like it; everything's within our collective grasp..."

When Alonzo called Monet ninety minutes later, she told him to pick up the items she had ordered at their favorite gourmet carryout place. By 5:30, they had all entrees placed on the dining-room table, with Electra seated between them. Electra spoke in Monet's direction as soon as Alonzo poured the wine.

"This is as upscale as my celebrity partner's place. I think you'd like her."

"Indeed yes, judging from what Alonzo and I saw when

Marne and you won. Perhaps you could give an encore to our ballroom dancing class."

"Sure, if I have time during this trip, but if not, we'll do it next time."

Everyone added to the pleasant conversation while eating; Electra steered to more serious issues after dessert.

"Alonzo and I will talk with China on Monday about her political projects, some of which coincide with some of yours. Would you share any details with me so I can have her follow up with you?" "Yes, and I'll start with Darla Tinibu. She's just as feisty mentally, but her health isn't. I hear rumors that other African power brokers have been approached by that shadowy Bigger Brother Conspiracy with lucrative offers if they cooperate to unseat her. I haven't detected any details, but I will need your assistance if the rumors come true."

"Just let me know and you'll have it. And from what Alonzo told me about Nila and Sanjay's behind-the-scenes work in Mumbai, you probably won't need my help building an African-Indian alliance. But if you do, just ask."

Alonzo glanced at his cell phone before saying,

"I think I better drive Electra home. It's been a long day, and she needs to rest up for Monday. You wanna leave now?"

Electra sent words in Monet's direction.

"Thanks again for dinner plus your diplomatic insights. And I'll tell China to keep you posted on anything she uncovers. OK, Alonzo, take me home..."

China didn't need to prepare for Electra's visit. They had set up one of the bedrooms when Zara and Amahl moved close to campus months ago, loading the closets and drawers with her East Coast clothes.

Electra awoke early enough for a half the normal distance run before having breakfast with China, who had Electra's favorite breakfast waiting. They swapped the latest personal stories and then watched a popular Sunday morning news show. Electra showered and changed into leisure clothes appropriate for warmer-than-normal temperatures. Afterward, she and China reviewed the consulting projects and rehearsed for tomorrow afternoon's meeting with Alonzo. She spent the rest of the day considering options for both upcoming meetings and shifting thoughts to LA.

Alonzo drove her to Eve and Nari's location. The sisters had hired part-time assistants to help during the morning, which meant they didn't mind the intrusion.

Electra kept it to a minimum by discussing business right away.

"It looks like your business has tailed off, but my LA consulting has caught on."

Electra stopped so Eve wouldn't have to interrupt, but this time Nari spoke before Eve could.

"That's good for you. Your dance routine really surprised us, but I've got my own for you and Alonzo that explains why I've been busy with something other than my holistic café. I'm pregnant."

The revelation surprised Alonzo more than Electra, who talked to herself while Alonzo quizzed Nari.

Alonzo didn't notice the weight gain; brothers never pay attention to how sisters look, but Alonzo does look out for their interests. I'll just sit and listen until they're all talked out.

Eve interrupted to stop Alonzo.

"Don't tell her she should go the vow-cer route. She and I can manage a unisex family containing twin boys. We'll borrow you whenever we need a male role model."

That brought Alonzo to a halt and let Electra start. "What's the due date?"

Nari snapped the answer. "Mid-December."

"Well, I think you'll do fine. Both of you are smart and mature enough to know what's about to start. And I have an opportunity that'll fit right in. Why not make a clean break with the past by moving to LA and expanding my consulting business? I've got Renee and a mid-twenties guy named Kai who run it now, and you two can grow it while teaching them more. And don't worry about all the relocation planning. Alonzo will do that."

Looking like the news had registered, he said,

"I can handle that. We've got a couple of months to plan for your arrival in California and--" Everyone expected Eve to barge in and she did.

"The arrival of my nephews. We know you can do it..."

The sisters needed to end the meeting so they could check the morning's business. Alonzo needed to get away.

Electra let Alonzo speculate as they drove to China's office, making only one comment as he parked.

"China has some news that'll turn Nari's surprise into an opportunity for you. Just listen to what she and I have to say." Alonzo looked like he might be ready for that.

China played its part by starting the meeting according to plan.

"I need to add a full-time political analyst. Eve and Nari are unwilling to help with the new projects I'm bringing in. Do you have any ideas?"

Electra's tone conveyed the optimism gained from the earlier meeting.

"I sure do. Alonzo's helping Eve and Nari relocate so they can work for my Los Angeles consulting business. He'll have most of the planning for that done by the time you hire someone. And Alonzo can get this office rearranged to hold the new person. In fact, I think he'll set up his own business in the space vacated by his sisters." Electra waited for China, who spoke as fast as planned to preempt Alonzo.

"That'll be a good move for him. And it's time we rename Kirchner Consulting. We'll do that when we hire the new analyst."

Looking expectantly at Alonzo, Electra gave him all the time he needed to compose his thoughts. When ready, he said,

"What should I call it?"

"You and I can come up with that when we get back from the Deus Lab."

"When are we going there?"

"After our meetings with Congressman Chaska and Professor Plannert."

"And when will those take place?"

"Between now and the end of next week. For the rest of this one, we'll be in Washington, following up on what China and I talk about next."

Alonzo looked like he had just been hit by one of Electra's patented info-overloads. China remedied that by saying,

"Let's celebrate by having some of the mood elevators I brought. They can serve as lunch…"

The forty-five-minute pause bucked him enough to be a good listener when Electra returned to business.

"China told me yesterday that Congressman Chaska has made inroads for me at Washington's Bureau of Indian Affairs, and she's already told Feather's Tribal Council that I'll accelerate progress building the National Alliance of Indigenous Tribes—aka the NAIA. I visited the major ones last year."

Alonzo's listening paid off. He remembered enough about tribal business to join the discussion.

"I didn't go, but Electra told me about them. She helped the Seminoles Project Director Dyani Hache in Miami and her counterparts Johana Maipetal in Albuquerque for the Navajos and Tanis Tuckahoe in Seattle for the Suquamish set up green energy and sustainable businesses. And I'm going to help run them, right?" "Correct, and we'll extend it to Alaska. These are more reasons why you need your own office."

"I'm starting to see how this all fits together."

"Excellent, and you might see more when we visit the Deus Lab next week…"

The rest of the meeting focused on politics and the November elections. After ending the meeting two hours later, she gave instructions to Alonzo for tomorrow.

"Please pick me up early tomorrow morning. We'll take our chances and drop in on Chaska."

"Got it. If you ride home with China, I can go now, OK?"

"That's the plan. See you at 7 a.m."

One of Chaska's eager young staffers met them at the security area a half-hour after the Ford Office Building had opened to the public. She knew that Electra was one of the Congressman's advisors and invited her to come to his office even though he was campaigning this week in Connecticut.

Electra thanked her but declined, instead making an appointment when he would be there next week. Alonzo had them driving away by 9:30 and asked for another destination.

"Professor Plannert likes to start early. I'll call him."

He answered, and by 10:30 she and Alonzo were sitting in his office. Electra had plenty of time, so she let Plannert wend his way through a courteous greeting before reaching his Environmental Scanning Committee.

"You said you'd call the next time in Washington, and here you are. I imagine you have a number of exciting new projects.

Perhaps one of them might be suitable for my GWU committee. What might you recommend?"

"I'm part of NASA's Antarctic Expedition. We're investigating sub- glacier lakes for new species and testing seabed robo-exploration and mining equipment. There could be many collaboration possibilities."

"How nice. My committee is currently preparing an ecological impact proposal for the International Seabed Authority. Might you provide a contact?"

"How about I have the Mission Director call you, and you can take it from there?"

"Perfect, and I will treat you to lunch after I tell you more about other GWU projects…"

Electra decided to let Alonzo work by himself for the rest of the week so he could plan for all the new moves. His only other assignment would be to drive her Sunday morning to the Deus Lab. She also worked alone and enjoyed withdrawing into her Fortress of Solitude while talking with Indira.

Indira already knew Electra's recent crop of DC accomplishments, as well as her intentions for visiting the Lab and Feather, but she waited for Electra to explain further. After she finished, Indira added even more.

"Your and Alonzo's planning is thorough, as is your purpose for meeting with Chaska. But meeting with Feather will be merely a brief courtesy call to keep her in your planning loop. However, your meeting at the Deus Lab will be the opposite. Do not ask me to elaborate. I do not wish to spoil the surprise. Please contact me on your drive back to DC."

Electra let Alonzo do most of the talking during the drive, adding comments only when asked. She smiled to herself when they reached the Lab after Alonzo said he was ready for anything; Electra didn't know if even she could handle whatever might be waiting inside.

Indy-M didn't keep them waiting. Taking them immediately to the robo-soldier and android fabrication area, she stood at attention before barking "ten-hut."

Electra looked long enough to figure out what she saw, but she wanted to hear what Alonzo's gasp meant. He gasped less than in previous revelations instigated by Electra or Indira, but it nevertheless showed his surprise.

He spoke after gaping for ten seconds at two groups of five robo-soldiers who had just snapped to attention.

"Well, I'll be… she's built our first platoon…two five-member squads of robo-SEALS, and I know what the names on their uniforms stand for. A-L and A-1 through 4 stand for Able Team Leader and teamers 1 through 4. And ditto for the Bakers."

Indy-M snapped back,

"And they'll call you Commander." "Do I get to train them?"

Indy-M said,

"I do that. I have the time and place. They'll stay here until you deploy them, but you must stay long enough on this trip to train their voice and surveillance software so it knows all about you." Electra pointed out what Alonzo's attention missed.

"And it looks like she's built clones of you and me. Let me guess their names, Electra-M and Alonzo-M."

The unnervingly lifelike androids stepped toward their human counterparts.

"Yes, I am Electra-M. You must take me with you so you can teach my personality software to be like you."

Alonzo spoke after Alonzo-M said much the same. "How smart are you?"

Indira's voice replied.

"I shall tell you all you need to know on the drive home. From now until tomorrow morning's Feather meeting, address your teams." "Roger that."

He and Electra followed orders.

Feather didn't detect Alonzo's impatience; only Electra knew why he hurried through his part of the even briefer briefing session, and she agreed they would stay one more day when he insisted he wanted it for drilling his squads. While he did that, she alternated between reviewing her Chaska meeting agenda and training Electra-M.

Electra invoked Indira's avatar once they were on I-95 and waited for her to speak.

"I expect you already know how valuable your android doppelgangers are. They are beyond what your mere mortal adversaries have. Indy-M has uploaded my most advanced neural-net control and personality software into the latest generation of Japanese androids that are built to look like you and Alonzo. You can virtually be in two places or do two things at once."

Electra asked Alonzo's question.

"How smart are they? Are they self-aware?"

"Decide for yourself. They have the same software that Indy and Jason-M have."

Alonzo pulled onto the shoulder before saying, "I'm gonna let Alonzo-M drive."

Alonzo-M followed directions all the way home.

Alonzo appointed M his permanent driver, which made for efficient travel to the Chaska meeting. Electra-M came too but stayed in the car with the driver. Electra introduced Alonzo as soon as they and the Congressman were in his alcove office, which guaranteed privacy.

"Alonzo is my logistics and security person. Both activities are increasingly important, especially for people in politics, and doubly so during campaign season. The polls say we're ahead, which means our platform promo-ads are working."

"And in no small part, thanks to you. You seem to know in advance where public sentiment is heading. A lot of my more moderate Democratic colleagues like our platform."

"What's your take on President Goodman? Are the polls right?"

"I think so. All the other candidates from the three major parties are straying too far away from the middle-class center. And rumors about any link to a Bigger Brother Conspiracy have no substance. So, if the climate remains like it is for the next five months, he might cruise to victory."

Electra segued, using the Congressman's last remark.

"Lots can happen between now and November. Let me explain what options I have for you…"

Alonzo had lots to say on the drive away.

"Monet would applaud your diplomatic machinations. He might add me to his security team if he wins, and that gives me an idea. You should tell Indy-M to build us a team of android secret agents. Our robo-SEALS look too intimidating. I can place them when I need them."

"That's a great idea. I hadn't thought of that, but I'll talk about it with Indira. And here's something I have come up with. How do you like 'Strike Force Security Services' for the name of your company?" Alonzo could barely control his enthusiasm.

"I love it, and it fits all kinds of security. We'll start with the 3-D World, but you can help me move into Cyberspace, OK?"

"I like your thinking. This has possibilities..."

Unlike Electra and her closest allies, Xinqian Hung didn't like what Zoltan Sultani was thinking, and she called him out during the Gang's latest conference call.

"There is too little disruption going on in America. You need to instigate more. What plans do you have?"

"I've already got one that's ready to take a bite in California out of the public's confidence. And I'm adding to it some climate change problems NASA's uncovering. All this'll strengthen the hold that Big Government and Business have around the world, and that makes us even stronger."

"Make it happen. I want to see and hear about it soon." Xing ended the call on that threatening note.

Chapter 11
July 2172

"Danger Lurking"

Electra took advantage of the relative calm in her professional and personal worlds by extending her stay in DC. Doing so allowed her to assist Alonzo while keeping close to campaign politics. Remote monitoring of the Antarctic mission worked too because no glitches surfaced that the Aphrodite software couldn't handle. And the same applied to watching over Renee and Kai, as well as talking with Marne.

She helped prepare Eve and Nari for their move to LA and told China she would make the final decision on her top analyst pick. Alonzo sent Alonzo-M to pick up the two Electras on that mid-month Wednesday. He and China were already at the office, waiting for the candidate.

Electra observed for a minute the candidate, who was calmly sitting in the conference room. She wanted to compare his resume with what she saw.

So, this is Jamison Brookheart. His looks match his bio-sketch: early 40s Black male with shortish hair and academic-style glasses fitting for his poli-sci degree from a top university. He's moved up the Washington reporting ladder, taking assignments across America and abroad. I'd better find out why he wants to change ladders.

Electra zeroed in on this after explaining her role and expectations. "You've built a successful career that has life in its legs. Why do you want to join China?"

"She tells me you've given her the green light to take this consulting business to the next level. I want to be someplace where

I can make an impact, help draw up a mission statement, and do analyses, write editorials, and hold interviews that cut through to the authentic issues."

"Hmm, that's what we're looking for. I have some follow-up

questions…"

Jamison's firm handshake and steady gaze when leaving the conference room told Electra he met her expectations. She told that to China before Alonzo-M drove her home, leaving his employment details and office setup in China's and Alonzo's capable hands.

Renee enjoyed having Electra's remote monitoring, and Noah gave her plenty of emotional support whenever needed. Thanks to his and Kaira's coaching, her serving and surfing skills kept building.

She and Noah were among the pairs of surfers practicing on a pleasant-weather Saturday morning when Kaira spotted danger. Her waving arms brought everyone onto the sand so they could hear her. "We can't surf here today. I just spotted a school of that new find of fish that's threatening the California coast. Did you hear about it on the news?"

One of the bigger fellows replied.

"Yeah, they're supposed to be a bigger piranha species migrating north from Brazil. And get this, you can pick up flesh-eating bacteria if they bite you." He ran out of words to say, but Kiara had more. "The wave-surfers are done for the day, but the pairs can still practice board balancing onshore. Why don't you split into pairs of two teams and help each other?"

While most of the surfers practiced or watched, Kaira hiked to the closest lifeguard station to report what she had seen. He said this was the first report at his beach before alerting other guards via a portable radio.

Renee knew more about piranhas than anyone in the group but didn't flaunt it. Instead of feeling frightened, she filed the incident away and would mention it to Electra if she brought it up first.

Electra had a good idea why Renee didn't pick up her call that evening.

Saturday night has always been party night for the young crowd. I won't advertise it, but I'll plan to call her on Thursdays. And the same goes for Kai, but I'll try Marne now.

Marne answered just before it exceeded the maximum number of rings. She sounded happier as soon as she recognized Electra's voice.

"Sorry it took so long to pick up. I invited over some of the show writers so we can add some scenes to the next episode. The director says we need to add more pizzazz and can use one of those ChatGPT apps if we need some ideas. I wish you were here."

Electra automatically switched to her consulting role.

"That'll work if you use the app correctly. It's all about dialogue management. Here's all you need to do… you'll get a dialogue box prompting you with a question, like 'What do you want to know' when you start it. Make a specific and detailed request for starters. And when it gives you a recommendation, you and your screenwriters can improve it before feeding it back in so it can make it even better."

Marne continued when Electra stopped.

"We'll do that right now. I'll tell you how it works when you call next week. I hope all is fine wherever you are."

"It is. We can talk longer next time. Bye-bye."

Electra talked with Alonzo a couple of days later, who didn't need any help but said she should call Eve for the latest on her and Nari's thinking about consulting in LA, so she did that evening. Eve's voice projected energy.

"I've heard a lot about Hollywood females starting families after putting off pregnancy when starting their careers, so I've been researching how the combination of vitamin supplements and exercise helps pregnant women. Nari's been my tester, and she tells me she's feeling better than before. She had severe morning sickness and cramps a month ago, but they've gone away. She's in month number four and is up and about. Her ob-gyn thinks my holistic approach is helping."

"Do you think moving after she delivers is better than moving before?"

"We think it's better to move ASAP. That way, we've got an obstetrician and hospital where we need them in the future, and I can start consulting out there sooner."

"Good planning. Please let me know if you need any help."

We will, but I think we can manage on our own. You've never gone through pregnancy, but I appreciate the offer. We'll keep you posted. Bye."

Electra said more after Eve disconnected.

She's right, but I helped dear Robin two lifetimes ago when she miscarried during the episode when muggers stole her van and shot her dog. What a ghastly mess a breech-block delivery can be. But she pulled through, and a year later I grew her twin daughters invitro after harvesting some of her eggs and fertilizing them with Matt Forte's sperm. I hope I never have to do any of that again. Well, enough about that; let's get back to the present.

Electra stayed happily busy, finding time to read up on women's exercising and nutrition. Her life coach clients might like her findings. And remote monitoring of the Antarctic Expedition remained trouble- free because the Aphrodite software performed flawlessly.

That's why a call from Britt surprised her a week later, and she let her lead the dialogue.

"We've got a problem. I wish the hardware functioned as well as your software, but it doesn't. Some of the seabed AUVs have stopped working; they're stuck in the ice or on the bottom. Are there any Aphrodite tricks you can do to get them working again?"

"I'll try, but there's only so much I can do remotely when it comes to hardware."

"That's why I'm calling. We might need you to come to Antarctica for a hands-on inspection. And you can bring Alonzo."

"When will you know if we're needed?"

"In about a month. We might get lucky as the Antarctic spring gets closer, but it's still two months away."

"Well, I'll make sure to be ready if you need us. Just keep me posted…"

Electra thought it wise to chat with Indira after the call.

Indira needed no prompting. She spoke as soon as her avatar appeared.

"I have been preparing something that will help you in both Hollywood and Antarctica. I'll mention the Antarctica overlap first, because Britt's call prompted you to call me. And of course, I understand the genesis of the organisms found in sub-glacier lakes.

I simply extended what Benoit Mandelbrot, the 20th-century maverick mathematician who popularized Chaos Theory and Fractal Geometry, based on Mandelbrot and Julia sets. Georg

Cantor first found it when he used Cantor sets to reach infinity, a number greater than all numbers.

"Mandelbrot used iterative self-similar computer algorithms to explain some patterns seen in Nature, all the way from living organisms like trees to the Universe. My fractal algorithms exceed those of mere mortals because they utilize the laws of physics that every process in Nature must follow if it wants to minimize energy consumption. I can even predict how these ocean creatures will evolve.

"And you see Fractal Geometry applications today in Hollywood's special effects as well as layered design patterns used in new clothing fabrics, but mere mortals cannot reach what I have."

Indira stopped to let the consequences of her words sink in. Electra talked a minute later.

"There are so many things we can do with this. You have to—" Indira answered the request before it came.

"No, I do not have to tell you more, at least not now. I've told you enough so you can impress your NASA people. You can also hint about fractal component design in nano-electronic applications. I will tell you more when you need it, but this is enough for now."

Indira left without saying another word, but Electra did detect her wry smile.

Renee continued smiling more than ever. Her expanded circle of friends, centered on Noah, kept her happy. Tonight's late Friday night roller skating outing along the Santa Monica Boardwalk would make her smile even wider. She had nothing but happy thoughts as she skated from the townhome toward the meeting location.

But happiness crowded out Electra's careful instructions regarding being out alone at night. Renee never heard the whirring rollerblades coming up behind her. Two hands shoved her off the Boardwalk and into a stand of bushes far away from the lights. Another pair flipped her onto her back. The guy that shoved her down now stood above and spoke ominously.

"We meet for the third time, and this time we'll make it stick by sticking it in you. Ready or not, here I come."

The guy who had flipped her pulled her halter top over her head, blinding her vision and muffling her screams before locking her arms in his. The other pulled her skating shorts down to her ankles and then leaped on top before punching her senseless.

Renee didn't know how long it took to come to, but when she did she knew what caused the pain she felt between her legs and the voices she had heard before. She managed to prop up on her hands and knees, but fell on her face when trying to stand. Shock and dizziness forced her to heave dinner, and when everything finally cleared, she pulled up her pants after standing and awkwardly skated home.

She showered to wash away the physical pain, but the anguish remained. She felt more than hurt; she felt violated. What would she say to her friends? Now that the evidence had been rinsed away, she couldn't prove who did this. Renee promised herself to keep it a secret, even from Noah, even from Electra. She would pretend everything is normal.

Renee turned off her cell phone before collapsing into bed. Only silent tears kept her company until she fell asleep.

Chapter 12
August 2172

"Back to Normal?"

The analytic part of the Electra-Alisha duo knew they should expect intrusions to disrupt what had been two months of uninterrupted progress. Eventually, they would regress to a normal state. Electra would have to come back to Washington for election preparation, so she returned unannounced to LA two weeks before the Labor Day weekend for unobtrusive in-person monitoring.

When the rideshare took her to the consulting office, she saw, the minute she walked in, Alonzo's meticulous preparation-at-a-distance for Eve's and Nari's September arrival. Two additional workstations awaited them, and Renee and Kai still had ample space, even though their workloads had continued growing.

Kai was out closing clients, but Renee rushed to her as soon as she ended the phone call.

"We didn't know you were coming today. Noah and I would have picked you up if we did."

"I didn't want to slow you down. How's everything?"

"Sort of hectic, but things should get back to our new normal when Eve and Nari get here. And after they settle in, you can talk with them and Kai about hiring Noah part-time. Kai could sure use him." "That will be a group discussion in a couple of months. But now, please tell me about the personal side of life…"

Electra helped Renee with office work while they talked, and by the time Renee drove them home, she felt that Renee and the consulting business looked even better than ever.

When Electra called Marne that night, she got even more good news.

"A local news show contacted my agent because the host thinks you'd make a great interview. She'd like you to talk about how you've done so much out here so quickly. Why don't we go out for brunch this coming Sunday and we can talk more?"

"That'll be perfect. I'll have the rest of the week to settle into my normal LA schedule. I'll pick you up at eleven..."

Marne announced the surprise waiting for Electra as soon as she came into Marne's house.

"My agent wants to join us right here so we can role-play your interview. She's already coached me on what the hostess will say. Let's go to the dining room so you can meet her."

Marne handled the introductions before the threesome ate while trading anecdotes. After clearing the table an hour later, role-playing began.

Marne started by saying,

"Our guest today is a relative newcomer to the LA scene, Electra- Alisha Kirchner, who wowed us on "Flirting with The Stars" when she and Marne Dionne captured the audience along with the first-place trophy. According to my vetting via her Trans-Astro Consulting Website, she came to LA to start the business. I love its tagline—AI- Empowerment for the Stars—and it offers a host of services, but I want to focus on her Life Coaching, so let me ask, how did you acquire at such a young age the skills to do this?"

Electra dived right into her interviewee role.

"I had wonderful mentors and coaches who encouraged me to use all my skills. That's why I established a Washington, DC consulting office handling socio-political and related services, which I extended into the services covered by Trans-Astro. And a business partner recommended I open a new office in LA."

The agent signaled for Electra to pause so Marne could continue. "And by taking that advice, life coaching has been your stellar performer. You told me backstage that most of your clients are women. Why is that?"

Electra had figured out the question-answer flow, so she said,

"Because LA women, and Hollywood females in particular, consider me a role model for self-empowerment to own your own life via clarity, confidence, and momentum. In other words, pick the right goals, develop confidence-building skills, and take actions that collectively build momentum."

Electra paused before the agent needed to signal.

"That does sound like a recipe for success. It should work for males too, so why are women flocking to you?"

"Well, the post-modern world recognizes female leadership and multitasking abilities. Historically, even America has been a patriarchal society, conditioning women to ignore how good they are and instead focus on taking care of others rather than themselves." "I see, and that adds to what you told me earlier. You teach your students that they should always do things that make them happy while at the same time moving them toward their goals. And the best way for this is to believe in a God of their choice, self-awareness, and free will, even though the latest physics and neuroscience, and Chaos theories say this might not be so. Did I state that correctly?"

"Yes."

"Well, let me ask some additional questions so our listeners will know how your life coaching services can make everyone happy, goal go-getters."

Marne's applause ended the role-playing, and her agent said, "You're a natural at this. You handled the introductory questions like you've heard them a jillion times. Answer any other questions the hostess throws at you like you just did, with brevity and authenticity."

"I will."

Marne shifted them back to right now.

"One practice run-through is enough, and it's made me hungry for more goodies. Let's grab some and then talk about other things." Electra relaxed while doing most of the listening, but she leaned closer when Marne leaned toward her.

"I have an actor friend who travels a lot, and when I told him about how good a life coach you are, the next time I saw him, he told me about someone who wants to meet you. His name is Dean Niles, and it turns out he's an air traffic controller working at LAX, and he'll give us a behind-the-scenes tour if you'll give him a life coaching session. If it's OK, I'll call to set this up."

"Did he mention what he expects to get from my life coaching?" "He says the nation's air-traffic-control system software is outdated. Its ChatGPT pieces are a couple of generations behind, and when you combine that with control tower understaffing, air travel hazards are increasing, and that puts more pressure on the controllers to collaborate more. He says your life coaching might help him handle both better."

"He's right; that's what it's designed to do."

"Well, he wants to give us a tour on an upcoming Saturday. For the next month or so, which will work for you?"

"I'll make them all work. Just let me know what works for you and him..."

According to Marne, Dean picked the second Saturday in September, which gave her ample time to rehearse for another J-Team episode while Electra did the same for her interview. Electra even had enough extra time to monitor some of the less important projects in all her worlds, but stayed deep enough in the shadows so no one felt she was intruding.

Electra and Marne waited outside her home for Dean to arrive. Marne moved toward his car as soon as he tooted the horn, with Electra just behind.

Marne managed the introductions while sitting in the passenger seat. Electra sat in back, listening to Marne's summary of her interview while sizing up Dean.

He looks pretty fit, dresses well, and sounds sharp for a mid-forties male, which are the traits a competent controller should have. This should be a good day for all of us.

After Marne completed her summary, Dean said,

"I've heard this self-help stuff before. Do you have anything practical to add?"

"I do. Here are some of the steps I add. Practice asking why not rather than why, and look for good enough, not perfection. Then take tangible action and embrace any fear or discomfort that comes with it."

"Hmm, what else?"

"Here's a framework you can use for doing this. Replace these old habits with new ones. The first is automatically reacting like you did before. Think instead of panicking. Here's what you do...be self-aware and jot down your thoughts and feelings. The next is telling yourself that what you want to do is too hard, or that you're not qualified. Do this instead...tell yourself anything worth doing is going to be hard because if it were easy, it wouldn't be worth much. And the last I'll mention is getting bogged down in minutiae. Take the big-picture 50-

thousand-foot view."

"I like it, and the 50-thousand-foot view fits where we're going." Electra knew she had said enough, but Marne added a final thought.

"Electra also told me I must always be true to my values and know where to draw the boundaries so I protect myself as well as others." That ended the conversation until they exited Dean's car, which was now occupying a restricted parking space. Dean led the way to a security van that took them past a couple of planes that were being prepared for departure and then toured a couple of runways before driving them to the control tower. Electra liked the jargon for referring to planes and runways.

Dean used his access card to enter, simultaneously walking and talking and adjusting his volume so it wouldn't interfere with the controllers.

"Towers today are standardized yet highly flexible, allowing for customizable colors and materials to meet the needs and reflect the local identities of their respective sites. They can be tailored to the local environment, taking into consideration seismic and climate, especially wind, rain, snow, and ice, and their height will depend upon each airport's traffic and sightline requirements."

"Today, we have them ranging from about seventy-five to almost two-hundred feet. The height will depend upon each airport's traffic and sightline requirements. And they can handle more flights, are more affordable, and easier to maintain..."

Electra listened long enough to Dean's explanation before tuning in to herself.

What a clear blue view on such a bright morning. No wonder the windows are darkened and the lights dimmed. The contrast sharpens the clarity of what I see outside. And what a view it is... I can see acres of planes leaping skyward or gliding to land on miles and miles of runways. The controllers have to focus and multitask while talking to multiple pilots and hunching over multiple monitors, watching plane-dots, and listening to background chatter. It's a young person's job... still more men than women. And Dean says they practice in a control tower simulator so no planes crash during their training. I bet AI-empowered software makes their job easier.

Both Dean and Electra soon stopped talking. His winding walk let them watch over the controllers' shoulders, but he froze when the power died, as did all the controllers. Emergency power kicked in ten seconds later, but it was just enough for exit lights and the critical monitor at each controller's station, the one showing the trajectories of all planes.

A din of noise kicked in as the controllers tried to manage visually the traffic, using their monitors while glancing out. Electra elevated to a higher state as soon as she saw the controller she was standing behind begin to struggle.

Saying nothing, she tapped him on the shoulder with her left hand before pointing on the monitor with her right hand's index finger to which planes would soon be in trouble. And she kept doing it until gunshots rang out, followed by one voice screaming,

"We're under attack; they're battering down the main entrance door."

All controllers jumped to their feet and started yelling and panicking. Dean and Marne gaped; the lightning brain elevated to its penultimate level.

Grabbing Marne's hand, Electra shouted,

"We're getting out of here right now," but Dean yelled back,

"We're supposed to stay here until security guards come. All doors automatically lock, and the stairway's too dark."

"Then you can stay, but Marne and I are going." Electra spotted the secondary entrance and stumbled toward it, never letting go of Marne.

When reaching it, the lightning brain took only seconds to memorize the wall-mounted stairwell chart. Electra then punched the emergency exit button before they disappeared into the stairwell's darkness.

Electra's catlike eyes and reflexes let her navigate better than Marne, so she slowed their descent just enough to keep Marne in tow. Marne was gasping five flights later, so she stopped at the next landing. She heard pounding feet and harsh voices coming up from below, but they disappeared when a door opened and then slammed closed.

Electra had begun trembling and gasping by the time they reached ground level, but she recovered within ten seconds and groped for an emergency button. But when she punched it, nothing happened. Feeling further, she found a wall-mounted cannister that had to be an industrial-strength fire extinguisher. She ripped it off the wall and used it to batter the door handle. Then she kicked the door open and pulled herself and Marne into the glaring brightness.

Electra remained motionless until her eyes adjusted. And when Marne's did too, she began pulling her toward the relative safety of a terminal nearly a quarter of a mile away. And what a sight she saw.

Gads, no one but us has escaped or is heading to the terminal. I see some guards unloading from two security vans and a chopper about to land. No one's looking at us…we're in the clear.

Electra saw a swirling mass of confusion when she and Marne entered. She grabbed onto Marne once more before pushing through the crowd and out an entrance. Then she shoved her into a cab and yelled before slamming the door.

"Go home and call Dean. Then call me as soon as you know how he is. And no matter what, I'll call you tonight after the late news." Electra took the next cab to the safety of her townhome.

She didn't expect Renee to be there, which was what she wanted. She needed time to decompress, so she ran until she drained away all the tension and emotional energy. She stood under the showerhead, still wearing her running shorts and top, until her brain settled into a more normal state.

Electra let Renee's call go to voicemail, and when she listened to it hours later, she had already guessed the topic.

She's staying at Noah's tonight. Good for them, and good for me. I don't want to explain my day.

Electra sat in front of the TV monitor, flipping mindlessly through stations until the late news came on. She knew what the lead story would be. Her favorite local announcer read it.

"All flights to and from LAX are still suspended. Local and national security agencies have now confirmed that terrorists staged a combination of Cyber and 3-D attacks, leading to the deaths of at least five people who were in the control tower and injuries to more. Names are being withheld to respect their privacy, and experts are working to verify the identity of the attackers. So far, none of the usual suspects have claimed responsibility…”

Electra called Marne as soon as she turned down the TV monitor’s volume. Marne spoke after the second ring.

“I’m so glad you called. I haven’t heard back from Dean. What do you think?”

“He might not be among the five people the terrorists killed or injured. Try again tomorrow. How are you feeling now?”

Fatigue tinged with relief came with Marne’s words.

“Grateful to you. Do you think we might have been killed if we had stayed?”

“Perhaps, but we didn’t, and we’re still alive, so let’s move on…”

Chapter 13
October 2172

"Where to Next?"

When Electra's cell phone awakened her from a rem sleep dream early the next morning, her first thought was as dark as her bedroom.

Only bad news comes this early. That must be Marne's news that Dean is dead. Well, let's face the facts.

She was right about the caller but not the news. Marne's voice sounded as relieved and happy as her words.

"Dean's alive. His gunshot wound and clubbing aren't fatal, but the trauma left him in need of physical and mental counseling. He wants you and me to come to his first therapy session, which is scheduled for Friday. I'll pick you up Friday morning if you will."

"Sure, that's the least I can do. How does eight sound?" "We can stop for a snack on the way. See you then."

Electra used some of her free time that day and next, preparing for the therapy session by reviewing articles and videos talking about why victims develop emotional attachments to their leaders or rescuers. She stopped when satisfied she understood the basics of the "Rescuer Trap."

Maybe Dean thinks he should have followed me to safety like Marne. If so, I better let my empathy lead to whatever he wants. I've worked for years making mine stronger. Today, I'm not an intimacy avoider, but I do like to have enough space. Well, I'll sit and listen and just follow the counselor.

Electra hid her embarrassment behind a bland smile when Dean rushed to hug her. The counselor, who fit the image of a female psychiatric counselor, separated them soon enough and guided Dean back to his seat at the table. Marne and Electra sat opposite him, and the counselor sat at the head.

Thirty minutes later, she summarized what she wanted Electra to do.

"Dean says you're a life coach. His insurance will pay for you to meet with him once a week, and the three of us will meet every two weeks. Does that meet with your approval?"

"Yes, and I won't charge anything. When should we start?"

"Next week, and it'll be good to let Dean handle the details so he becomes less dependent."

"I understand; I'm sure he will too as we proceed..."

When one of the local networks used Dean as the human centerpiece for a follow-up story about the airport attack, he praised Electra's life-coach consulting, mentioning her uncanny ability to lead people to safety, as well as her Lightning Bolt gambling app. And when he said he wanted to take her to Las Vegas, one of the airlines offered to cover all their expenses.

Picking the date took precedence at the first meeting they held at Electra's office, and Electra agreed the Halloween weekend would be fitting, but she might have to reschedule if other events intervened and took her elsewhere. The rest of the session focused on helping him learn her techniques for collaborating with others.

When Britt's phone call came in a couple of days later, Electra knew this might be one such event but let Britt tell her where she might soon be going.

"We'll be leaving for Antarctica before Thanksgiving. We've got you slated to be part of the team for fixing the seabed AUVs while another is looking for correlations in volcanic activity between Mount Erebus and volcanoes just west of Anchorage. And a third team's looking at correlations between Antarctic storm parameters and those we see on Mars. Don't you have devices that forecast eruptions and storms?"

"Uh, one of my contacts does. If you like, I'll see if she'll lend them to you."

"Great, and we'll pay whatever the rental fee. Keep me posted on the devices, and I'll do likewise on departure to Antarctica."

Electra invoked Indira's avatar as soon as Britt ended the call. Indira waited for her to state the problem.

"Commander Starling wants to borrow the Seismic Shock and Storm Predictor apps I built with your and Indy-M's help a couple of years ago, but catastrophes destroyed both. Do you suppose you could replace them?"

"I can do more than suppose. First, let me scroll on the monitor their GUIs.

The first one appeared seconds later. Seismic Shock Predictor

Input: Big Data _____Proprietary Data _____

GPS Location ______Depth _____Radius _____

Minimum Intensity Level: __

Date/Time Interval: Start ____ End ____

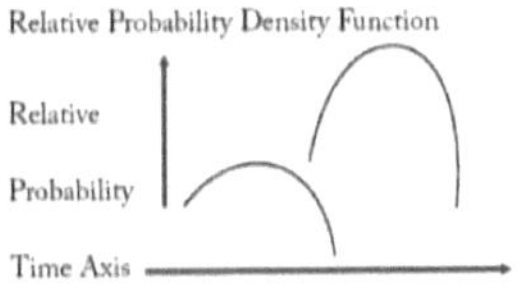

Relative Probability Density Function

Relative

Probability

Time Axis

Relative Probability: _____

(Equals RPDF integrated between Start and End)

Note: Seismic Levels: Light (4-4.9) Moderate (5-5.9) Strong (6-6.9) Major (7-7.9)

It took only seconds before Electra said,

"That's what I used a couple of years ago, and it sure helped me avoid the worst of the Yellowstone volcanic eruption back then." "And here's the one for storm forecasting."

Its GUI scrolled a moment later. Severe Storm Forecaster

Input: Big Data _____Proprietary Data _____

GPS Location ______Storm Cell Radius ____

Minimum Level: ____

Date/Time Interval: Start ___End ____

Atmospheric Parameters used: Temperature Pressure Humidity Wind Speed Rotational Velocity

Vertical Wind Shear Electric Potential Diff.

Relative Probability Density Function

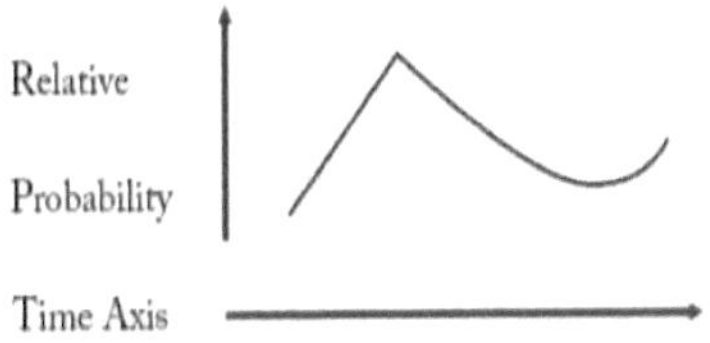

Relative

Probability

Time Axis

Relative Probability: _____

(Equals RPDF integrated between Start and End)

Note: Storm Levels: 1(75 mph) to 5(160+ mph)

"That's the one Alonzo used to get me out of the Kansas tornado."

Electra waited for Indira's avatar to tell her more, and from her wry smile, she knew she would like it.

"Indy-M and I will reconstruct them and upload our next-generation software. But don't tell your Commander Starling too soon. Keep her waiting so you can avoid the ratchet principle. Indy-M will send them to you or directly to NASA. The choice is yours. Let me know what you want."

Although Indira's GUI vanished before Electra could thank her, words weren't necessary.

Nothing else came up that would interfere with the Las Vegas weekend, so Electra sat back and let Dean handle the details.

But Dean wasn't the only one planning Las Vegas details. So was Zoltan Sultani, who always followed stories involving Electra. Dean's interview ignited his desire to get her Lightning Bolt gambling software, and it took him only minutes to arrange for covert CIA agents to "chat" with her during her Las Vegas trip. He looked forward to the outcome.

Dean's weekend plan began unfolding soon after he and Electra checked into the hotel on Friday afternoon. The concierge arranged for an early evening tour of the Las Vegas Strip, using a battery-powered vintage Cadillac convertible. The driver gave a non-stop monologue of the sites, but Electra preferred listening to herself.

The Strip is even more spectacular than when Tim and Kwame visited for the Cyberspace Expo several lifetimes ago. That time, I prevented Darla's Cybergard security team from pirating their laptops and stealing my software they tweaked while working in Austin for Hud. This trip should be less stressful.

The warm breeze flowing softly through the enormous back seat added to her total immersion in the moment.

Las Vegas is still the center in a constellation of worldwide gambling and adult entertainment centers. Macau in China, Manila in the Philippines, and Dubai in the UAE can't match what I see here.

Traffic on the boulevard-like Strip flowed constantly, unimpeded by stoplights or cross traffic. It had wide sidewalks carrying tourists of all nationalities and ages spanning thirties to sixties, toting shopping bags. Curbside pylons protected them from cars, and a low-slung wall on the other side displayed electronic billboards.

Street lights weren't needed; the glow from the horizontal lights between the floors or the video-gilded surfaces of magnificent casino hotels gave plenty. The welcoming signs of restaurants and entertainment clubs, plus the light-spangled drive-up casino entrances, added to the electric ambiance, and in places, the lights from an overhead walkway descended like starlight.

Electra lost track of time, but when the tour ended at a 1890s-style ice cream parlor near their hotel, she was happy to devour a hot fudge sundae while admiring the authentic-looking tables, lights, and uniforms. Las Vegas magic had brought the past into the present.

High Noon Saturday marked Dean's main event. Dean would play Blackjack with Electra at his side, giving him advice. And neither Dean nor the casino surveillance system knew she had an advantage. Earbuds connected her haptic glasses to the cloud so Indira could see all the cards dealt, turning her into the Singular card counter, able to beat the casino no matter how many decks the dealer's shoe contained. Indira's reassuring voice told her what to do just before they took the final space at a table.

I will tell you the best bets to make, and I expect you will use them and small amounts of money to win gradually so Dean can remain inconspicuous. And there is no need for me to wish you luck because the odds will be in your favor.

Electra could tell as both the minutes of play and Dean's chips piled up that the casino's glitzy lights shining down and glamorous people streaming by simultaneously thrilled and stressed him, even though he took her recommended beverage break each hour. He decided to cash in his chips at 5:30 because he had won enough and had an evening event scheduled after a light snack at their hotel.

The concierge had booked seats to a Las Vegas retro-pop star show at the Las Vegas Cybersphere Theater, which meant the Alisha personality would accompany Dean. As they walked into the 360-degree video dome interior, she sensed from the crowd and lighting that the performers would exceed her expectations. And they did. The virtual reality combined with special effects to once again bring the past into the present.

Although Electra concealed it, her cumulative time with Dean was beginning to bother her. She needed time alone, so she cheered to herself when Dean announced his intentions for Sunday at a mid-morning buffet.

"I'd like to play the slots and craps by myself until we leave for the airport late this afternoon. Will you be OK on your own?"

"Sure. I can check out some of the amusement parks. Why don't we pack after brunch so we're all set to get to the airport. What time's our flight?"

"It leaves at 6:20 and should land at about 7:30. So, let's meet back in our room at five."

"Good, and good luck to both of us…"

While waiting for her cab, Electra toyed with the idea of visiting a sensual massage parlor for a three-person experience but talked herself out of it.

My sex drive is cooler in my present lifetime; I think it's morphed into cerebral friendship and caring, and the change is safer and less draining emotionally. I can handle that…

When Electra explained to the driver what she was looking for, he began listing his favorites.

"Our amusement parks have the best rides anywhere, and their names say why. We've got the Inverter, the Bigshot, and the Slingshot rides guaranteed to give thrill-seekers all they want. And our twisty rollercoasters, like the Canyon Blaster, El Loco, and Insanity might shake your brain loose, but I would pick the Take Your Chances coaster. It loops together two independent multi-car trains. It usually looks like they're gonna collide."

"I'll take your pick. Please take me to that park…"

Electra decided to reconnoiter the place by warming up on less jarring rides, and while walking around, her lightning brain's warning system issued an alarm. It had detected two "too normal" male tourists lurking in the background ever since Friday's arrival, but Electra had been too preoccupied to notice. But now she did.

Why would someone be following me here? It has to be connected with Dean's interview that mentioned me. Could they've been hired by a gaming software competitor who wants to steal my apps? Or maybe a jealous life coach? I better stay alert.

Electra kept thinking while walking a circuitous route and stopping occasionally to gaze in directions that kept her followers on the fringes of the views. They were always there. By the time she reached the Take Your Chances roller coaster, she was ready to do that, literally and actually.

She bought a two-ticket ride and then sat in the rear car. Her followers sat only several cars ahead, but at least she had an easier time watching them. And on the first loop, she looked for jumping- off points if she needed to take evasive action.

When the ride ended, Electra stayed put, using her second ticket. When the followers saw that, one rushed to the ticket booth while the other moved closer. Both were in place when the train glided away.

Electra's lightning brain made its first move at the top of the second incline, which had to be hundreds of feet high. The train had slowed enough for her to grab onto a support beam and swing out before it started plunging again.

But she nearly fell because her coordinated muscles didn't have as much snap as only a couple of years ago. She shinnied awkwardly toward a lower place where she could make her next move. It put her hanging onto a beam ten feet above a horizontal stretch of track where the second train would slow before dipping and accelerating, and as it came into view, Electra knew what to do.

She timed letting go so she could drop close enough to an empty seat in the middle car. She nearly bounced off but managed to pull herself in by locking onto the safety bar. After doing so, she stayed fully engaged to the end of the ride. And once there, she disappeared into a crowd before anyone could stop her.

Electra kept moving all the way back to the hotel room while watching for her followers, who never came into view. Then she grabbed a Coke from the refreshment bar and collapsed into a chair by the window. By the time Dean arrived a little before five, she knew what to say when he asked about the amusement park. "There were lots of great rides, and the Take Your Chances roller coaster gave me the biggest thrill. How'd you do at the casino?"

"I lost a little playing craps but won a little on the slots, and overall, this has been a great change-of-pace weekend. I'm all set to get back into my routine. A brief change of pace is what I learned from your life coach program. And I'm also ready to grab a snack before we head to the airport. How about you?"

"Sounds good, and then I plan to sleep on the flight all the way back to LA."

"I think I'll do the same. And let's grab that snack at the airport. I'll feel even better knowing we're there."

"I agree, so you lead the way…"

By the time their flight reached cruising altitude, Electra had already settled into a more relaxed mental state and began thinking ahead.

Only Indira will ever know about the roller coaster incident. And I think I know where I must go next, but I'll stop thinking about that until tomorrow. Until then, I'll just be thankful that when I took my chances, the odds came up in my favor. That's something to savor.

Electra did that all the way to LA.

Chapter 14
November 2172

"More Places to Go and Things to Do"

No unforeseen events accompanied Electa's return to LA, which meant nothing interfered with her preparations for her immanent pre-election trip to DC. She made sure that Renee and Kai kept the LA consulting office perking along, and attended all Dean-related meetings.

And the day before her Sunday flight, she called Eve and Nari. Eve picked up right away.

"I know you'll be busy with electioneering, but say hi to Alonzo and Monet for me if you have time."

"I'll make time, and I'll be back in time to help you prepare for Nari's delivery day. Can I say hi to her?"

"Sure, she's right here."

Electra could hear a muffled argument before she started talking in a tone that couldn't completely cover her irritation.

"Hi, Electra. Have a safe trip and don't worry about my delivery preparation. My ob-gyn has told Eve and me all we need to know, and don't worry, I'll be back to work by January, which no doubt will make you happy."

"It will, but the most important thing is your twin boys' wellbeing." "It's mine too, and Eve pitches in. And that's about all from here, so I'll say goodbye."

Nari hung up abruptly, but by now, Electra didn't let it bother her too much.

Unlike Electra, no one ever hung up when Xing was leading a Gang-of-Three-Plus-One encrypted phone meeting like the one occurring late that very same Saturday.

Zoltan listened but would not talk unless asked.

Xing rattled off what he already knew she wanted, and when she asked him about the presidential election, he spoke confidently.

"I have orchestrated all the steps you wanted that will assure Goodman will get elected. And that is good for us."

"I hope so, and I hope you will find out how Electra Kirchner avoided your covert CIA agents. She's elusive."

"She is, but I have other means for observing her, which I will continue doing."

"Please do, and do not disappoint me." Xing terminated the call.

China surprised Electra by picking her up at the airport. Knowing they could use the drive time to talk about more personal topics before turning to consulting issues later, she waited for Electra to start.

"How's the two-office setup working? Does Alonzo lend you Robin and Matt whenever you need assistance?"

"Yes, but I've streamlined the place so I'm pretty self-sufficient. And on the political consulting, you're as close as the phone."

We'll talk more about that after tomorrow's TV interview. I'm all set, so tonight we'll just take it easy."

China's glance told her there might be more than kidding in what she was about to say.

"Easy for you isn't the same as for most people, but I'm glad we have similar work ethics."

"And that's why I'm glad you're working here..."

Driving to the broadcast studio by herself, Electra arrived two hours before airtime, which pleasantly surprised the host. He and Electra had his script ready by the time the "on air" sign flashed.

"Our next guest is Electra Kirchner, who is speaking on behalf of Congressman Benjamin Chaska. According to what we've already heard about him and his platform during the campaign, he's a liberal-leaning Democrat that middle-class voters like because he supports compromise rather than polarization, dislikes both Congressional and Supreme Court Legislative Privilege, advocates for government-funded college scholarships promoting sustainability and environmental studies, and champions the cause of Native American Indians per the National Alliance of Indigenous Americans—aka NAIA— which positions America's longer-term leading role in the fledgling Indigenous People's Worldwide Alliance—aka—IPWA. "Welcome, Ms. Kirchner. Did I state his position correctly?"

"Yes, and thank you for including me on your show."

"You are most welcome. I like what he says, but we've heard social change promises like these before, and they never seem to come about. Why should we trust him?"

"I would ask the same question if I were you, and my answer says he and his campaign are both transparent and authentic. You'll see what we're doing because of our Social Change Leadership Model. May I summarize it for you?"

"Please do."

"Thank you. We call it our 'Seven Cs,' which we group into Individual, Group, and Community. The Individual comprises the Conscious self-awareness of beliefs, values, attitudes, emotions, and actions, plus Congruence and Commitment. The Group covers Collaboration, Common Purpose, and Controversy controlled by Civility. And the highest C is Community, which means all members have the same Citizenship."

Electra stopped right there, waiting for the host to respond. He didn't smile, but he did move closer before saying,

"This has possibilities. Tell me more."

Satisfied five minutes later, he shifted subjects.

"What does the Congressman say about International Politics and Defense Spending?"

"He has learned the lessons of history taught through the ages. Great world powers have great responsibility to maintain world order via diplomacy rather than military might. That's why he wants our president to maintain a dialogue with China. It's clear that China wants to dominate the technologies that will fuel economic and military might, and they are biotechnology, artificial intelligence, and quantum computing."

"That's what President Goodman promotes. Would you care to elaborate?"

"Wars of the future will be hybrid affairs, meaning they will use unconventional weapons leading to asymmetry between offensive and defensive capability. Defense will employ a hedgehog concept that gives it a decisive advantage in all theaters, namely land, sea, air, Cyberspace, Outer space, and Social Media Space."

"What do you mean by unconventional weapons?"

"AI-controlled drones, robots, and super-soldiers. Stealth

UAVs and AUVs. Robo-suicide terrorist squads. Surveillance, sensors, and jammers. Open-source big data analyzers. Nano-based 3-D printing. Shall I stop here?"

"Yes, but what about the human factor? Will ChatGPT-like software make political and military leaders obsolete?"

"It's possible longer-term, but for the time being, humans are better at collaborating, morale-building, planning, and training because our empathy lets us communicate, implement, and adjust better because we can see other points of view, no matter the context."

"Well, we are out of time, but this is a fine place to end. Thank you, and best of luck to Congressman Chaska."

Electra's cell phone chimed on her drive away, signaling a call from China, who spoke as soon as Electra gave her normal greeting. "Great job. You always speak with authority that draws people in. The Congressman will be pleased. I'm sure it will convince any still-undecided voters to vote for him, adding to what the polls say about his likely win. Will you be at campaign headquarters on election night?"

"No, I told him you'd be there instead because my work is done. Go easy, but hint about accelerating IPWA and NAIA activity next year." "I'll do that. So, where are going next?"

"I'm off to see Alonzo and Monet. You take care for the rest of the day, OK?"

"Will do."

Alonzo had a selection of his and Electra's favorite mood elevators waiting for them in his conference room, and he guided her there as soon as she walked in. Her look told him she needed to decompress, so he led the conversation.

"Monet did my listening and says you made a convincing case for Chaska's domestic and international positions. I knew you would, just like I know you'll have everything ready when we head to the Antarctic. Anything new coming from Britt or Boomer?"

"No, you know everything I do. And I'd like to work out of your office until I fly back to LA. I won't be in your or your robo-SEALs' or secret agents' way if I do, will I?"

"Not at all. I keep them elsewhere until needed, and you'll be able to see how well Robin and Matt are functioning. And they'll stay at China's office when we're in the Antarctic."

"Good thinking."

"When are you heading back to LA? Are you gonna visit Professor Plannert before you leave?"

"Thursday after the elections. And I'll call Plannert tomorrow…" Electra kept the Plannert conversation focused on Antarctica after the Professor's pleasant greeting.

"What were the results of the call from the Expedition's Mission Director?"

"He liked our ecological impact proposal, so we'll do pertinent data analysis on what's collected."

"Excellent, and when I come back to DC, I can brief your Committee."

"We will look forward to that. And please be careful. NASA missions always have high risks…"

As she expected, the election risks went Chaska's and Goodman's way. Electra flew back to LA early the next day.

Electra went directly from the airport to the consulting office; she sensed from Renee's look that something was amiss. Renee let her know even before welcoming her home.

"You better call Eve. She and Nari are at home, and Nari's not feeling good."

Electra didn't bother to talk when Eve answered her call. She could tell from the primal screams in the background that Nari's third stage of pregnancy had suddenly become much less than good.

Electra yelled to Renee after ending the call,

"I'm taking the van. Get a ride home from Kai," before charging to the van and then racing into the midst of an emergency that might be the same as the one from several lifetimes ago now streaming through the lightning brain.

I've heard screams like that only once before. They came from Robin when I helped her survive a breach-block delivery. I can't say any more until I see Nari.

Electra double-parked at the apartment entrance, then pounded on the door enough times for Eve to hear her over the screams coming from within.

Eve's look of terror required no words from either.

She charged into Nari's bedroom and saw the cause of the screams. Nari lay on her back in a welling pool of blood, chest heaving from labored breathing. Electra pulled the sheets around her and then heaved her off the bed and into her arms before carrying her to the apartment entrance. Eve hadn't moved but did manage to say as Electra struggled past,

"What's happening? Where are you going?" "To the closest E.R. I'll call you when I know."

The attending E.R. doctor took charge as soon as he spotted a blood-spattered Electra and an almost-comatose female in her arms. He gave commands while pushing toward her with a gurney.

"Put her on the stretcher and follow me..."

Electra did as told and then stumbled to a nurse's changing station, where she dabbed blood off her clothes before washing it off her face and hands. Then she collapsed into a waiting room chair.

An E.R. nurse woke her up two hours later.

"Your daughter pulled through. Eclampsia triggered early labor, and it was messy, but you got her here just in time. We managed to save one of the twins. Congratulations, you now have a grandson." Electra roused herself well enough to stand and thank the nurse before saying more.

"No-no, I'm not the mother, just a friend. Here's the name and phone number of her sister. Please call Eve."

Electra drove to her townhome to decompress by grabbing a snack and then going for an endorphin-generating run. By the time she finished, she knew what to do next. Calling Renee, she spoke first. "Nari's OK. She gave birth to one boy who's a month premature but looks healthy. Please call Eve and congratulate Nari for us."

"I will? Where are you?"

"I'll be working at home for the rest of the afternoon. Bye for now." Electra busied herself with Antarctic preparations until she grew hungry enough to make a light supper after putting work away. She didn't expect Renee to come home early. She would probably visit Nari first.

Electra was watching a new episode of a popular action-adventure series when her cell phone chimed. She recognized Eve's number, but Nari's emotion-laden words streamed out.

"Yeh-you saved my son. I can never repay you, but-but I promise to be nicer. I never realized until now how much you give to me and Eve."

Electra lightened the mood by filling in where Nari left off.

"You and your sister give me a lot, too. And I'm sure that you and Eve will make a great home for your boy. Is it OK if I call Alonzo? He'll want to hear the good news about you and his first nephew. He's now an uncle."

"I'd like that. And I'd like you to be his godmother. Will you do that for us?"

"I'm honored. It's like sharing virtual DNA. Now you and your son should rest up and let Eve take over. Sleep well."

Electra did the same.

Chapter 15
December 2172

"Departing Preparations"

Electra had already reviewed all but one item in her Los Angeles personal and professional worlds to confirm that they needed no tinkering before departing to the South Pole. She had saved the favorite for last, her singular friendship with Marne, who invited her to a one-on-one Sunday mid-afternoon lunch at one of her favorite destination restaurants. Electra had dressed for the occasion, and even though the maitre de's manners were nonchalant when taking her to Marne's table, she could see that the pair impressed him. Electra returned Marne's two-handed greeting and smile before sitting opposite and waiting for Marne to speak.

"I'll miss our chats while you're on your Polar Expedition. I don't suppose you'll be back until January at the earliest, but your Life Coach program gives me enough to do on my own until you return." "It's designed that way, and thanks to you, my LA client list continues growing."

"All I do is tell my friends who are looking for some help that you're the best, but I can't tell them why, other than I feel you really care. Maybe you can give me a better answer.

"How about I do that after we order a drink?"

Marne followed every word when Electra continued ten minutes later.

"Unlike many Life Coaches, I take a practical and pragmatic approach that doesn't get my clients bogged down in theories or ideas. And I say that, when interacting with the American culture, you should accept the notions that there might be a God, free will might exist, and we might have a spiritual consciousness separate from the brain. Think of this as Mind-Brain duality, which has been with us since the ancient Greek Philosophers. And remember that contemporary America is willing to accept others if they reciprocate. "And I also say you should be skeptical of the hucksters spouting the latest fantasy theories about the Universe, Quantum Physics, and the Theory of Everything. It's OK to listen, but always remember that what they say has zero impact on everyday life, and a growing number of scientists say their theories are full of holes, and I don't mean Black Holes."

Electra paused for Marne to comment.

"I don't worry about any of that, but you do such a nice job connecting Philosophy, Religion, and Politics. How do you manage that?"

"I've studied enough about each to understand how Political and Religious leaders use only the ethics piece of Philosophy when dueling to control what people think and do. You can track this back two thousand years to when the Church and State first emerged. And today, even though the manipulation techniques are more sophisticated, their intentions remain the same."

"You articulate your position so clearly, but I guess that's why you're my screenwriting coach too. Well, when you come back, I'll have more prospective clients for you."

"And I'll have some additional topics for us to discuss. Here's a teaser. I'll introduce you to the four horsemen of the New Atheism, Chaos Theory, and Robert Sapolsky-like neuroscientific complexity, deconstruction, and emergence. But that's enough until I come back."

Electra had nothing to worry about before leaving for Antarctica, but Renee looked ready to ask a question or two that might surprise her, so she waited for them to come while the two were sitting alone in the consulting office.

"Eve and Nari tell me something I already know, you're really smart. But they say you know a lot about socio-politics and can connect it to science and philosophy and religion when talking about the world's two Superpowers, the West led by the U.S. and the East led China. I asked them to tell me how you do it, but they said I should ask you. Can you give me a summary?"

"Sure, and I'll need to sketch a diagram while explaining, but I'll start by saying I study history through two POV lenses—Neuroscience and the Physical World. Neuroscience says all people are pretty much the same genetically via shared DNA. But different prehistoric tribes developed different civilizations because they invented different Myths, Superstitions, Religions, and Philosophies to explain the 3-D World they inhabited. And as they struggled against weather and stronger animals to survive, they developed unique Scientific, Political, and Economic systems leading to urban- centered Nation-States that grew by exploration and exploitation, conquest and colonization."

Electra waited for Renee to say something; she did while slowly nodding her head.

"You packed a lot in, but I think I understand." "Good, now I'll sketch a diagram."

Electra talked a couple of minutes later while pointing to her diagram.

The World's Political Order

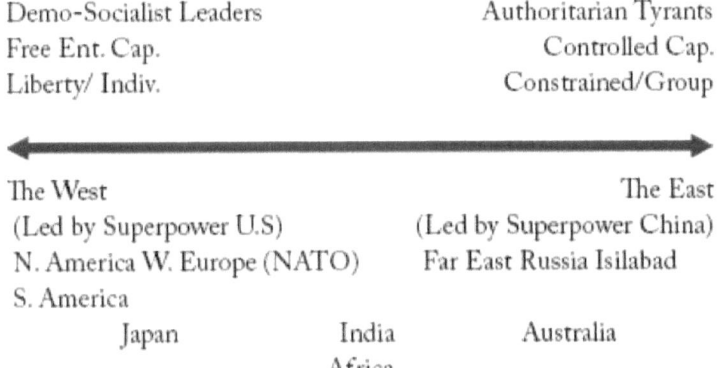

Demo-Socialist Leaders		Authoritarian Tyrants
Free Ent. Cap.		Controlled Cap.
Liberty/ Indiv.		Constrained/Group
←———	———	———→
The West		The East
(Led by Superpower U.S)		(Led by Superpower China)
N. America W. Europe (NATO)		Far East Russia Isilabad
S. America		
Japan	India	Australia
	Africa	

"I plot each nation's location along an axis, with the U.S. at one end and China at the other. And the other nations are spaced along it according to their locations relative to the ends. This should be pretty clear to you."

Renee nodded silently, so Electra sketched again before talking.

Orientation to History's Timeline

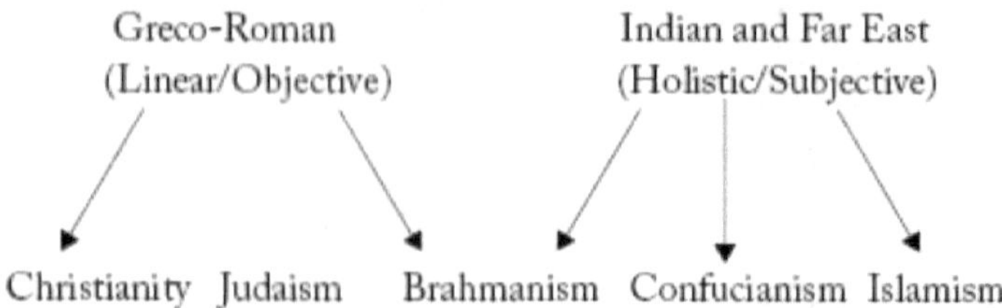

Revolutions:

- Tool/Weapon-Making Farming/Domestication Writing Transportation Bureaucratic Military Printing Scientific Industrial Electronic Computer Information A.I. Software
- **Each Civilization Adapted Differently**

"And here you see how different religions view history's timeline. Linear means beginning, middle, and end, or birth, growth, decline, and death. Holistic means when something dies, it's reborn.

And always remember that every nation today, no matter how noble or nefarious their deeds seem, pales before those from the past. Ancient China invented paper and gun powder, and built the Great Wall. Egypt built the Great Pyramids, and Rome engineered the Aqueduct.

"But Roman Legions murdered millions, and Rome crucified or fed Christians to the lions in the Colosseum to entertain its people. It was their low-tech version of today's Virtual Reality. And hordes of Huns and Mongols killed everyone and burned everything in its path, and those coming behind them eventually toppled the Roman Empire with the sword or decimated the population with the Bubonic Plague. Despite our best efforts to be kinder and gentler, human nature all too often has its way."

Electra could see from Renee's look of horror she had gone too far, so she backtracked as best she could.

"You're mature enough to understand the truth, but maybe I've emphasized the negatives too much. I should have recited a couple of positives, like vaccines and non-invasive surgery.

You've thought about most of this before, so please don't fret too much about it.

And at least now you can integrate everything into an entire socio-political worldview."

Renee straightened up before saying,

"I won't. Maybe we can talk about it more when you come back, and until you do, I'll tell Eve and Nari. But don't worry; I won't unless they want to hear..."

Nothing worried Electra during the flight to Antarctica. She had flown over all other continents, experiencing African herds flowing over endless plains, sands blowing over interminable Middle East deserts, and South American emerald tree canopies stretching to the four horizons, but the pristine whiteness of the Antarctic glacier, punctured by jagged mountain peaks occasionally jutting out and framed against a celestine blue sky, gave her a sight to behold.

The C-17 transport's altitude kept her from seeing the only form of life that might be moving below, but her imagination could see columns of penguins trekking away from the coast after leaping out of the ice-blue frigid waters. And Electra could barely feel its gentle touchdown on a multi-mile-long runway etched on the snowpack as it coasted to a stop at the turnaround point. The crew from a caravan of snowcats and trailers unloaded cargo and passengers, then prepared the plane for its return flight. Even in the spring season, planes always left as soon as possible.

Britt and Boomer greeted the NASA people once they entered the research station and waited until everyone collected their gear before taking them to the unisex dormitory. They would collect the newcomers for a tour before dinner and a briefing session with the entire team afterward.

Electra put herself in Britt's group, listening more to herself as they walked.

This place looks just like the videos I watched. It's a multi-level marvel of high-tech equipment and high-touch comfort built into the glacier. Today's Antarctic explorers and researchers have it so much easier compared to those who came before, but that's what progress has always done. And way back when, you can't miss what you never had. But I'm glad I'm living now and not then.

And she talked to herself while falling asleep that night.

The briefing session told me nothing new. I already know what I'm supposed to do. And I'm ready to go. Indira and my lightning brain make it so…

Chapter 16
December 2172

"Survival Above and Below"

The weather forecast for the two-hour snowcat drive to the AUV launch station reported only moderate blowing snow conditions, which meant no special procedures would be needed. Near twenty-four-hour daylight meant that the snowcat drivers simply needed to let their eyes glance only occasionally at the GPS homing beacon dot.

Electra sat in the lead cat next to the driver, trusting the forecast to hold at least until they reached the station, but the weather changed abruptly. She could feel when touching the windshield the temperature diving, and the ice pellets pounding on it obliterated all sound almost as thoroughly as the billowing vortex of what looked like steam erased everything from sight. Electra thought the driver should slow but he didn't, and she could see that the snowcat had begun deviating from a straight line. A crevasse appeared in front before the driver could react, and when it plunged in, her scream might have been heard in the cat right behind.

By the time Electra and her fellow riders clambered out, the occupants in the other cats were huddling close to the crevasse. Her driver, the most experienced in the group, had hit his head on the windshield, adding to his confusion, and she sensed from the collective babbling that confusion reigned. The lightning brain switched to a higher state; Electra took control.

"Everyone, stay put. I'll get a rope from the trailer." Electra spoke again only minutes later.

"We'll trek from here to the station. Everyone, grab onto the rope and space yourselves out. I'll take the lead."

Panicky questions cut through the howling wind. "How far… how long?"

"Three miles, more or less. And we keep going until we get

there. Keep the tension in the rope tight. That'll help me keep us going in a straight line."

Not even Electra thought to radio their predicament to the station, but she didn't need to. She knew what to do and kept talking to herself while pulling the group forward.

Get with it, soldier; this is not a drill; it's life or death. Thanks to the tension, I can lean into the wind, and that helps me gain traction as well as watch my boots and GPS monitor. Just keep pushing ahead…

Their trek for survival ended three hours later when Electra pulled the last exhausted researcher through the station's double-door entrance, where station technicians cheered their arrival as well as their survival.

Station personnel took them to a dorm area where Electra and the arrivals unpacked gear and changed clothes before resting until the station director summoned them for a meal followed by a tour, and once again, Electra was suitably impressed.

And after the tour, he called an all-hands meeting to review what would start the next day, which began with his introducing Electra and Alonzo.

Electra sat stoically, thinking to herself while Alonzo smiled and waved back.

Britt didn't do it deliberately, but she's turned me into a celebrity. Well, at least my actions have made her words ring true. But now I have to match them with what I'm supposed to do here. I better pay attention to what he says.

The director did that next.

"While she's here, she and Alonzo will dive beneath the glacier, using our research AUV to get one of our exploration vehicles unstuck. And once that's done, she'll upload the latest Aphrodite software into our network so we can better analyze seismic and weather data. And while we're doing that, she and Alonzo will prowl as deep as possible beneath the glacier, looking for exotic sea creatures or whatever else is down there. So let's review our procedures and get set for tomorrow…"

Alonzo dropped through the research AUV's hatch before swinging into the pilot chair and buckling in. Electra followed a moment later, strapping into the robo-arms and searchlight control seat next to him. Two technicians sealed the hatch, and

Electra issued the command for Alonzo to activate the water propulsion drives. Thus began their search underneath the glacier.

Electra kept a stream of words flowing to keep Alonzo focused on steering.

"The searchlight beams spread out about the same as the laser blasters… that's why I have to keep panning them to stay away from the cracks and crevasses. No wonder the vehicle wedged itself into a spot the current Aphrodite software couldn't handle… steady as she goes… I'll tell you when to turn."

Alonzo's watchful eyes needed little help, so Electra changed her monologue.

"The bottom of the glacier looks like an inverted Antarctica surface and just as jagged. The current's too slow to wear away the sharp edges… and I can see what look like Jonah's icefish. According to one of the NASA videos, they have clear blood containing antifreeze compounds; evolution equipped them for this deep freeze… hey, I spotted something. Veer ninety degrees starboard."

Alonzo spoke ten seconds later.

"Great catch. It jibes with the intermittent homing signal when its battery gens enough juice."

Three minutes later, he asked for her next command. Electra activated the rear camera monitor before saying,

"Pivot 180 degrees and come to a stop about half a robo-arm from its stern." Electra said more when they were in position.

"I'll use the robo-arms to connect the sterns with a towing cable. And when that's done, I'll tell you to power up the drives so you can tow it back to our launch point."

"Now I can see why it's stuck. Its propulsion drives are bent backward into the ice. But that's OK for us. I'll be pulling the other way."

Alonzo nudged the throttle just enough to free them and then pushed to three-quarters thrust before steering a course for home.

But as soon as he did, the nose of his AUV pivoted upward and the one being towed began sinking, pulling them down into impenetrable blackness.

Alonzo didn't panic. He jammed the throttle to full power, but that merely slowed their relentless descent, so he asked for help, which now came from Electra's elevated brain state.

"The technicians didn't calculate the thrust correctly. Our propulsion drives can't deliver enough."

Electra could now hear Alonzo's panic that she was starting to feel. "Geez, now what?" The lightning brain shifted even higher; Electra shouted,

"Blow the ballast tanks."

That action tipped the resultant forces in their favor. Ninety minutes later, after the technicians secured both vehicles to the launch point, Alonzo and Electra climbed out.

Electra led the succinct debriefing session. The director spoke fifteen minutes later.

"Outstanding work on both your parts. Quick thinking kept you from sinking to the bottom."

Electra waited for Alonzo's humor to kick in.

"And if it hadn't, we'd be standing on the bottom. The AUVs can withstand the pressure below, but us humans can't survive."

Electra waited for the chuckles to subside before saying,

"And tomorrow, we'll head back down to see what sea creatures can, isn't that right?"

The director said he couldn't have said it better.

The next day's launch was even smoother than the first, and Electra gave the first command five minutes later.

"Steer toward the ocean floor and follow any creature that looks strange. And that's my last command. Yesterday showed how well we work as a team, so trust your instincts, as will I, and let's keep a dialogue going."

"Will do, and I hope we find something to catch for you to take back for more study at the Pequot Lab."

"Me too. I'd rather work there on my own. I like all the NASA techies and managers, but I think I've done enough for them."

"I like all but one, and you know who he is, but I'll follow your lead and keep being nice. No sense making him even more suspicious." "Good, and let's look for some nice specimens..."

Electra kept the searchlight beam panning as Alonzo steered a meandering path taking them down. And his comments about the Antarctic deep were almost as sharp as Electra's.

"There are more schools of fish down here than I thought we'd find. Whatcha think is swarming around us?"

Electra had been studying it, so she answered immediately. "They're krill that got here from the surface. They eat phytoplankton that are under sea ice but not glaciers. There's no light down here for them. If the krill weren't here, we wouldn't find any creatures because they're the primary food source."

"What about thermal vents? Couldn't they provide nutrients and energy?"

"You've learned a lot. They could, and if we come across one, maybe we can collect something from it…"

Electra and Alonzo kept trading comments for the next hour. Alonzo's boredom began to show until she yelled,

"You're steering us into—" The collision's jolt stopped her words. Alonzo's started seconds later.

"It's got its tentacles wrapped around us…What is it?" The searchlights showed Electra enough for her to yell,

"It looks like a cross between an octopus and a squid. But what's it doing?"

Electra saw the answer moments later when her searchlight revealed the cause.

"It's protecting its offspring from that prowling humpback whale. Kill the prop drives and let's see what happens."

Their AUV coasted to a stop just before the whale attacked. The octo-squid used only two tentacles to fight back because it didn't want to let go, so Electra decided to even the odds.

She jabbed at the whale with one of the robo-arms, but the humpback bit it off. Undeterred, Electra escalated her choice of weapons by using the laser blaster. That got the whale's attention; several additional hits drove it away.

Alonzo's excitement showed in his voice. "You won; now what?"

"Take us back to our launch point so we can bring in the samples we just collected."

"You gotta be kidding. Your so-called octo-squid is too big."

"No, I mean the smaller offspring. I'll use the remaining robo-arm to scoop them into a collection net. Be quiet while I concentrate."

As soon as Electra completed that task, Alonzo yelled,

"I'm gonna radio the docking station so they know what we're bringing back. And have you been recording all the action?"

"Yes, we have proof even if the big creature jets away."

Neither Electra nor Alonzo spoke again until the docking station responded to the call signal.

"This is docking station. Please report, over." Alonzo said just enough to astound them.

"We'll have our lights and cameras on for your return. Your ETA is in forty-five minutes. See you then, over and out."

Ninety minutes later, Electra and Alonzo climbed into the station after the samples had been stored. The director ran the briefing session as soon as Electra and Alonzo had changed.

"Great teamwork all the way around. We've got our videos and yours plus your samples, so here's what's next. After a meal, all of us will prepare for your final exploration tomorrow. You'll head toward the ocean floor coordinates we want you to investigate. Someone or thing is digging down there, and we want you to find out why…"

Alonzo needed no instructions at the start of their third descent, but it did trigger questions he directed at Electra.

"How did all this water get to Earth?"

Electra knew from previous study of the Solar System.

"It's the result of the Sun pulling Jupiter into orbit, which in turn pulled the asteroid belt. The asteroids contained water trapped inside, and they pelted into the earth for millions of years. And when the surface lava cooled, tectonic plate shifts triggered volcanic eruptions that spewed gasses, dust, and water vapor. Climatologists call this the 'Great Deluge' that led to water cycling between the oceans and the atmosphere. That's one of the reasons NASA studies weather and climate change."

Alonzo added more.

"Maybe life came already embedded in the asteroids. I bet that's another reason why NASA is always looking for places in our Solar System containing water."

"Yes, but let's focus on the water right around us…"

Electra used the searchlights to watch the ocean floor looming up as they approached the target coordinates, but Alonzo's voice shifted her attention.

"SONAR's picking up a torpedo coming at us," and his piloting shifted their AUV into a twisting spin parallel to the bottom. Electra could see it whoosh by before exploding on impact with the floor.

Electra didn't dare interfere with Alonzo's SEAL training, which he yelled while maneuvering.

"It's gotta be a Russian Military AUV. They've got more speed and firepower than us. How about I fake them by pretending to flee while drawing them in? When it's close enough, hit'em with your laser blaster."

Electra stared at the monitor as the enemy's dot closed the gap while she readied to fire, and she did so twice, seconds after Alonzo inverted and veered upward. She saw both blasts penetrate the windshield of a Russian AUV that took it to an explosive crash landing.

Neither Alonzo nor Electra spoke until he was piloting away from the blast site.

"We've survived enough action today to exceed even my quota of thrills. I'm taking us home to our docking station before something else starts chasing us."

Electra kept silent while considering other options.

The director, holding a private debriefing for security reasons, told them what he wanted to do.

"I'll send your videos to Commander Starling. They prove the Russians are mining down there, and that violates the International Antarctic Ocean Treaty. I'll tell her to use NASA's military connections to slow them down.

"And that's not all. I'll tell her you two made such an impact while here that NASA should hire you to train more teams."

The director's words provoked a reaction he didn't expect. Alonzo backed away from Electra, whose stare told the director he better not dare if he wanted to avoid trouble now hanging in the air. But she controlled her temper well enough to make a civil reply, accompanied by a faint smile.

"Thanks for the compliment, but we've survived enough challenges on this expedition to earn a trip to someplace safer."

The director knew better than to disagree.

Chapter 17
January 2173

"A Return to Safer Places"

Though grueling, Electra used the two stops on their three-leg flight to care for her octo-squids that she would take to her Deus Lab soon after returning to Washington. She and Alonzo napped enough during the flights to drive to the Lab only two days later.

Alonzo drove while Electra outlined what they would do.

"I'll put you in charge of finding a water tank contractor who can retrofit all our aquarium tanks with refrigeration units while I shop for live krill and mineral additives that'll make a pleasant home for our specimens. And then, I'll train Indy-M for taking care of them in my absence. Have I missed anything?"

"Nothing other than rocks and sand on the bottom. Plants don't grow where they come from, and you better equip it for total darkness unless you plan to experiment on their adaptability."

"I will and I'd like to if I can make time for it…" Electra paused to redirect her thoughts.

"And while we're here, you and I will make a courtesy call on Feather Trueson before meeting with Congressman Chaska to discuss the serious stuff…"

Indy-M took the pair on a walk-thru inspection after Electra placed the octo-squids in a small aquarium and added enough ice cubes to satisfy them. Then she drove to the marine shop in Stonington that she had been using for her previous ocean pets. Alonzo came along while making calls on his cell phone, but one of the marine shop employees said he could fit the tanks with refrigeration units.

Five days later, the aquariums were fully operational, and Indy-M knew how to keep them running and the octo-squids happy, so Electra and Alonzo drove to Congressman Chaska's office in Hartford after a quick visit with Feather.

Chaska complimented all the campaign work she had done to get him reelected, before asking what he could do for her.

"Just keep pushing the domestic piece of our NAIA and IPWA agenda to Congress and Indian reservation states. Alonzo and I are setting up an international recruiting trip to the safer places. And here's something about Russia's international meddling Alonzo and I just discovered."

Alonzo picked up precisely where Electra had already told him. "Russia is mining the Antarctic Ocean floor, which is a violation of the International Antarctic Ocean Treaty. We gave the evidence only to NASA, and they'll share it with their DOD contacts, but you're in a position to apply political pressure."

"So, I've got the scoop on what'll become classified data. I like that. Tell me more so we can coordinate what we'll be doing..." Electra and Alonzo had accomplished everything they had planned for this trip, so they split the drive-time back to Washington that afternoon, enjoying the splendid silence. Alonzo dropped her off late that night at China's before driving to Monet's. China welcomed her home.

"Where do you get all your energy to get so much done in so many places? I'm glad your cell phone works in all of them. Otherwise, you wouldn't have been able to let me know your whereabouts." "Alonzo's a big help. And tomorrow morning, he'll meet us at your consulting office so we can give you some of what we discovered that your clients might want."

"Then let's say goodnight so I'm ready for the information."

Electra detected a touch of fatigue in China's voice, so she made tomorrow sound lighter.

"And please don't worry, you'll be safe because I promise not to turn it into an information overload."

Electra liked Alonzo's take-charge attitude at the meeting, which let her listen more and talk less. China made a list of items she would share with the appropriate clients, and when Electra said maybe they could provide leads for co-research support, Alonzo had an even better idea.

"Why don't you call Plannert? His Committee is perfect for this. You said you'd do that the next time you're in town."

"Let's drive to his GWU office instead. He should be there, and he might treat us to lunch if we tease him with the right info. I'll let you do that."

Alonzo had learned from Electra how to turn the rigors of their Polar Expedition into a travelogue, especially the part about seeing exotic sea creatures.

"Why don't you talk at my Committee Meeting next week? One of the members might like to study your octo-squids."

"I assume it's the same time and place next week. If so, Alonzo and I will be there."

It was, so Professor Plannert began the meeting by introducing the guest speakers. Electra then summarized their role in the Polar Expedition before letting Alonzo dramatize the edited details. Both of them fielded questions afterward until Professor Plannert pointed to the newest addition to the Committee and said,

"Perhaps you might like to combine your cephalopod research with what Professor Kirchner is planning for the new species she brought back."

She jumped to her feet and said,

"I would be honored. We can study how the Antarctic's harsh climate caused it to adapt genetically. I'd like to compare its intelligence to other cephalopods, which rivals that of the smartest vertebrates."

"That's a novel research topic. I have contacts at Woods Hole, which is close to where I keep my specimens. Alonzo will make all arrangements as soon as you are ready."

"Thank you so much." She sat but rose before Plannert could adjourn the meeting.

"Do you suppose Professor Kirchner could give us a comparison between analytic models of the brain and generative large language models? I've never heard a talk or read a white paper that made it comprehensible."

Electra could feel her brain shift gears and spoke before Plannert could ask.

"Let me diagram on the whiteboard a model that fits both before I summarize the differences."

Electra completed it in less than five minutes.

Network Model

Process

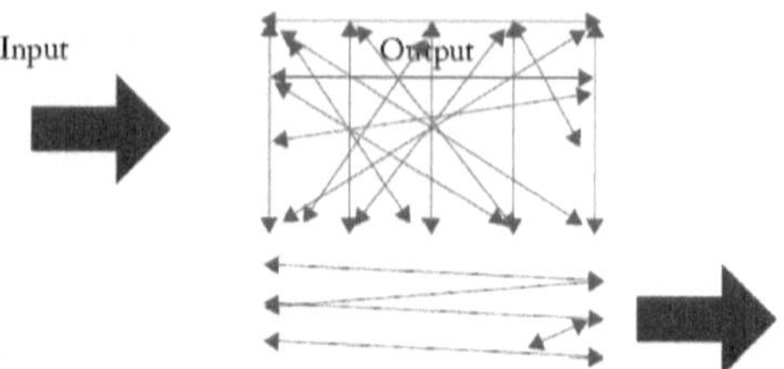

"The major difference lies at the line intersections. For brains, clumps of brain cells sit there, but for large language models, computer chips are there instead. And now, I'll bullet-point the differences."

For the Organic Brain Network:

- Input comes from all the Senses (Taste, Touch, etc.)
- Axons and Dendrites process them by communicating via electrochemical signals weighted according to what the Synapses have learned. (Cellular Microtubules contain Boolean Logic molecular structures).
- Output consists of new electro-chemical signals sent to the brain, organ, and muscle regions.
- Consciousness and Self-Awareness, Emotions and Feelings, Physical Movement and Chemical Output emerge.

For the Generative Computer Chip Network:

- Input comes from information coded as zeroes and ones.
- Computer chips process them per their algorithmic learning via Big Data.
- Output consists of new (generative) information coded as zeroes and ones.
- Consciousness and Self-Awareness, Emotions and Feelings emerge.

BUT PLEASE NOTE:

- **Both Brains and Computer Chip Networks are predictive calculators via pattern matching.**
- **We can't compare Human Consciousness and Emotions to what Computers might have. Carbon-based Substrates (that's Us!) and Silicon-based Substrates (that's Computers!) have different languages.**

After finishing it, she stood to the side of the whiteboard and faced the table before speaking again.

"I won't pretend any of this is easy. It isn't, but why don't we let the Committee hold a discussion sometime, using my diagrams?" The members traded uneasy glances until Professor Plannert gave everyone an escape route.

"Excellent suggestion. I'll let them decide how to proceed while I take you and Alonzo to lunch."

Alonzo was the first to speak after he and Electra drove away afterward.

"Where to now, Boss?"

"Please take me to the airport. I'm tired and ready to fly back to LA."

"Don't you need to go back to China's and pack something?"

"No, that's one of the joys of having multiple residences. I can just get up and go and leave everything behind. I didn't pick up any new assignments on this trip, but I'm leaving a couple with you. I didn't overload you, did I?"

"Nope, they just add to my job description, and there's no one else I want to work for."

"Please change the 'for' to 'with.' You've learned enough for me to promote you to partner, so get new business cards."

"I'll give the first one to Monet."

"She should be the first to know, even before Eve,

and you should be the first to tell everyone at our LA consulting office."

"I'll wait until you settle back in."

Alonzo waited for Electra to reply. She didn't, so he said,

"If I leave you at the airport, you can fly standby. I've learned from you the art of resting while waiting."

Electra used his words so each could withdraw into their private spaces.

"That's just one of the reasons I promoted you. And I'll practice resting, starting right now."

Electra napped on the flight, but roused herself one time to think more about Alonzo.

Of all my clone children, I never thought Alonzo would become closest to me…resets can work both ways. I can try to make changes that reset the 3-D World, but its events can reset me and my relationships. And for me and Alonzo, it's all been good.

Electra's happy thoughts stayed with her for the rest of the flight.

Chapter 18
February 2173

"Unsafe Places"

Noah couldn't read Renee's expression while she was peering at what could only be her cell phone's latest text message, but when she looked up, he guessed it might be good news, so he leaned close for her to tell him.

She talked just loud enough to keep it private.

"I can't stay with you tonight. Electra's returning tomorrow morning, and I want to tidy up her townhome."

"You want me to skate home with you? Some places along the path are unsafe at night."

"No, I know the way. When you catch up with the group, tell'em that's where I've gone."

Noah's hug was just enough to show his concern without knocking her off balance.

"I'll call you when I get home. Stay vertical."

Renee smiled as she roller-bladed away. The warm breezes added to her pleasure of thinking about Electra, but the combination distracted her. She never heard the skates coming from behind. Her only warning came from someone crashing into her lower back, bringing intense pain before she hit her head and passed out.

When she came to, she knew what damage had been done.

I've been raped again, but this time I don't know who or how many did it. No taunting words, but no extra blows. I'll shower when I get home and throw away these clothes. And I'll tell no one, ever.

Renee hid her feelings when Noah called.

"I got home fine, and I'll get up early to clean the place."

"Call me after you and Electra get back to normal. The three of us can have dinner here, and I'll do the cooking."

"She'll like that. Me too, so we'll catch you later."

Tears and comforting thoughts of the two people she loved the most carried her to sleep that night.

Everything seemed even better than normal when Electra arrived mid-morning. The townhome and Renee appeared to be spotless. After trading stories all through lunch, Renee called Noah to arrange for supper at his place, and when hearing their plan, she insisted on bringing dessert.

Electra loved listening to them talk. What they said complemented the body language she read.

Their personalities mesh…they are so comfortable with one another…their caring shows. I won't tamper with their relationship. She can stay overnight whenever she wants.

Electra's early morning visit to the consulting office found Kai reviewing two new projects with Renee and Noah. After sitting with them for only fifteen minutes, she knew all was in order, so she told them to carry on and went to talk with Eve and Nari, who had just arrived.

Carrying her now three-month-old son, Nari positively glowed when she met Electra more than halfway.

"Elton, say hello to Electra. She's your godmother."

Electra felt parental-like love welling up as soon as Nari placed him in her arms. She drew him close, making the instinctive sounds mothers make when cuddling their infants. Eve said nothing when she approached until Electra handed the infant back to Nari.

"I helped pick the name. It's the neatest one closest to yours. Nari insisted we name him in your honor."

Electra felt another emotional jolt, but this one she hid behind her words.

"I'll let you tell Alonzo about this new name, and I think he might be calling soon. He also has one. Please let me know when he does. We'll talk some business after that…"

Electra went back to the townhome for her morning run and worked pressure-free from there for the rest of the afternoon, calling Marne while munching on a peanut butter-covered banana. Marne recognized the caller I.D. and greeted her on the third ring.

"Electra, you sound alive and well. When did you get back?"

"Yesterday, and I'm fully adjusted. How have you been?"

"Doing fine, thanks to your consulting guidelines. A guy I used to date called me not long after you left. He noticed how good I'm doing and asked for my secret. That's when I mentioned your Life Coaching. Well, he said he'd like to meet you. Why don't I arrange for the three of us to go out for dinner? What days might work for you?"

"How about Friday?"

"Unless Troy can't make it, I'll let him pick the place, and I'll pick you up at 6:30. See you then."

Electra luxuriated in her reduced-stress schedule, finally realizing how all the pressure that her too-full schedule perennially placed on her had short-changed what she really desired. She had done it for so long she needed to reacquaint herself with what she wanted, and she was beginning to feel comfortable doing just that.

Marne gave while driving all the background information Electra needed about the fellow who would be buying them dinner.

"Troy Shandell used to be a rising Hollywood heartthrob thirty years ago, but his ego-filled womanizing tripped him up. He hit on me a couple of times when I was breaking in, thinking I'd be an easy mark for an older guy with a suave style and only slightly fading looks that made him so easy to fall for.

"But I resisted the temptation, and I think I popped his inflated self-image when I told him his too-fast hands and hairy chest turned me off, and I wasn't the only one to notice how he calmed down soon after, becoming a nicer person, and that's extended his career. And we've been casual friends ever since."

"Did he tell you what he's looking for from my Life Coach program?"

"He said he'd tell us at dinner."

Troy's mannerly appearance matched some of what Electra had surmised from Marne's sketch, but his body had become puffy in the wrong places and his dyed hair didn't match his face. His charm, however, remained.

He directed the conversation toward the ladies, asking them about their current activities, favorite foods and drinks, and what they wanted to accomplish this year. He ordered for each person, and recommended an after-dinner drink that all three ordered: an Amaro Sour.

The Alisha personality knew from a previous lifetime all about alcohol, but tonight she was only an observer from the shadows.

Electra waited for the Amaro Sours to arrive before broaching the life coaching topic. Troy replied wistfully after a second sip.

"I should have started taking better care of my mind and body twenty years sooner. If I feel good, I want to live beyond the century mark. Some Life Coaches say they can make it happen. Maybe you can help me by sharing your secrets. They seem to be working for Marne."

Electra knew he expected her to reply, so she let her words flow with confidence and care.

"The secrets are known to everyone who stays alert to the cues we get when comparing our current self with the one faded by the calendar. Stay active physically and mentally. Read and play a musical instrument. Emphasize relationships with people, pets, or causes to fight loneliness and boredom. Eat modestly. Have less meat and more fruit and fiber."

Electra stopped for Troy to comment, but Marne did first.

"That's the obvious part of Electra's Life Coaching Program. I think her emphasis on having daily goals and doing the things that make us happy sets her apart. She also says we should be nicer to ourselves, get rid of self-imposed guilt, and not worry about being perfect or what other people think might be our vices, you know, like indulging in food or sex or drink We're OK as long as we stay within our personal guardrails.

"If we live like this, we're living in the moment and life isn't a chore but instead a joy. Living longer comes with all of this, and if we don't live in the moment but try to postpone life for later, we'll miss living, because the present is all there actually is."

Electra spoke as soon as Marne stopped.

"Now you see why Marne is my favorite client." Troy seemed impressed.

"Then I would like to be your next favorite. When can you fit me in?"

"I'll call you Monday so we can pick a time that fits both our schedules. And to repay you for this lovely dinner, our first session will be gratis."

"Why thank you. And on that pleasant sentiment, I think we should adjourn."

Troy didn't need to signal the waiter. They simply got up and left. Electra decided Troy had prearranged for the charge to go on his tab.

Electra cruised through most of the weekend, expecting no calls. She knew what Renee and Noah were doing and had picked potential Troy meeting dates, but Alonzo's animated voice coming through on a late afternoon call while she was snacking in the kitchen alerted her to changes.

"When Feather called me yesterday about your ambassador role, I told her about the trip starting in Africa I was setting up, but she said she had a place closer to home, Alaska. She gave me all the contact info and said he'd like us to visit right away. He'd tell us what's on his mind when we get there.

"So, here's what I did. I delayed the Africa junket and booked flights to Anchorage from LA. It leaves at noon and gets in at six, so I can give you more details during the flight. Whatcha think so far?" "What should I pack?"

"Nothing. Just wear a warm coat. We'll buy what we need when we get there."

"Where will we meet?"

"At the gate. Print your boarding pass when you get to LAX. I'll Email your confirmation info."

"OK, partner, nice work. I'm in, and I'll catch you there."

Electra left a couple of voice messages that night before going to bed at her new normal time.

Waving when he spotted her, Alonzo jumped to his feet and waited for her to sit next to him. She gave him a partner-like hug and then sat down. Alonzo did likewise and then waited for her to explain why Renee was with her.

"I thought Renee might enjoy seeing Alaska, and she jumped at the opportunity when I told her you have everything set up. All I had to do was buy her ticket. You've learned all my tricks for travel planning, so I'm going to sit back and let you tell me what's in store."

"I'll start right now. We'll meet with Miki Chubbuck at his Anchorage office. He's the leader of Alaska's largest tribe—the Yupiks—and likes what the NAIA has to offer.

"And here's a snapshot of Anchorage. With a population of 300- thousand, it's Alaska's largest city. The second and third, which is Juneau, the capital, each have only thirty-thousand.

But all of Alaska has only three-quarters of a million."

"Haven't its volcanoes and seismic activity been acting up lately?" "Yes, and the second largest earthquake ever recorded destroyed much of anchorage in 1964. It registered 9.2, only a tenth of a point lower than the 1960 quake that struck somewhere in China."

Alonzo paused for a question he saw coming from Renee. "You think we'll be safe?"

"Sure, Alaska's so big and has such small cities, I don't think anything's gonna fall on us..."

Renee had the middle seat during the flight, and Electra listened intermittently to her and Alonzo's chatter, but paid attention when he described what he saw as the plane descended toward Anchorage.

Renee asked,

"Who's the airport named after?"

"Ted Stevens, one of the first and longest-serving senators." Alonzo said more while gazing out the window.

"Except for all the buildings, the Anchorage landscape looks almost like the Antarctic. And there are no tall buildings. I guess there are too few people to need-em."

Renee asked the final question before they landed. "Where are we staying?"

"At the historic Anchorage Hotel. Get set for some fun..."

The fun began late the following morning at Miki's office, located within walking distance of the hotel.

As Alonzo handled the introductions, Electra sized up Miki.

He looks just like I pictured an Alaskan native, big and rugged looking, and his jolly-looking daughter does too. I'm sure he has a good story to tell.

Miki took the group into a cozy conference room. He and Alonzo sat at the ends with Renee and his daughter, Lusa, sitting across from Electra. Miki's booming voice filled the room.

"Feather says you're like Native American ambassadors, and our tribes like the idea. We have a population of a little over 100 thousand scattered into about 225 tribes, many living close to Anchorage, but some in cities so small they all fit in one apartment building. We can use your help connecting with other Indian tribes across the lower forty-eight and figuring out the best way to deal with Washington."

Alonzo spoke when Miki stopped to catch his breath.

"Our NAIA can do that. I work for Electra and coordinate with Feather. What's the issue with DC?"

"It's got too many organizations trying to help us. There's the Bureau of Land Management and the Department of the Interior. Then there's the National Park Service and the U.S. Fish and Wildlife Service. They do know we've got lots of national parks, wildlife refuges, and natural resources, but they don't seem to know much about how our we're organized."

Alonzo used Miki's last comment.

"If you'll explain it to me, I'll tell my contacts in DC."

"The climate's too hard for tribes to live on reservation land, and we're all grouped into regional Native corporations or villages. Only our most famous people, you call-em Eskimos but we call-em by their real name—Inuits— still live near the water. Whenever you see wintertime videos about-em, you'll know why they're called 'World's most extreme survivors. It's just like Antartica."

"Electra and I were there a couple of months ago, so we appreciate what you're saying. And it looks like Anchorage knows how to handle snow. We walked here on plowed sidewalks and streets. There are people walking to tourist shops and buying Reindeer Dogs from vendors."

"Lusa will be your tour guide when we're done, and she'll tell you what's in-em. And now, I'll tell you why you see so many people out there. What do you know about Alaska's gigantic winter tourist attraction, the Iditarod Trail Sled Dog Race?"

Renee spoke before anyone else could.

"Electra and I watched a video about it, and she told me the word 'iditarod' comes from tribal languages and means distant place."

Miki and Lusa looked at her; Lusa said,

"You're pretty smart. Where do you come from?"

"I grew up in the Amazon Rain Forest. Electra says Amazon tribes are related to yours."

"She's smart too, and if put on some weight, you'd look sort of like me. But unlike us Alaskan natives, where you come from, you don't want extra pounds."

Miki took back control of the conversation.

"You'll be even smarter if you listen to me. The Iditarod is the celebration of our Native Alaskan spirit, and it's not about one musher against another, but man against Nature. Our people have been using dog sleds for thousands of years."

Whispers traded with Lusa had made Renee positively chatty.

"I like the name 'musher.' It sounds right for someone pushing a sled through the snow."

"They don't push. They've got a twelve-to-fourteen team of huskies and malemutes special bred and trained. We call-em athletes, and if you ever saw-em up close, you'd see their livin the dream. They love it, even though they burn up over ten-thousand calories a day." "Who can be in the race?"

"You gotta be at least eighteen and in good standing with the Race Committee. Parta that means finishing a previous Iditarod or two qualifying races of 500 miles each."

"That's a total of one thousand. Is that because the race is that far?"

"You sorta got it. The Iditarod goes from Anchorage to Nome. The straight-line distance is about 550, but the road distance is 1150, and the Committee plots a different course each year. That's why you can't compare winning times from one year to the next. And snowstorms do it too."

"What do the finishers get?"

"The first one gets a new truck and cash, and the last gets a red lantern. All others get bragging rights, which is a big deal up here." Renee's questions brought one from Alonzo.

"We're here now. Any chance we can see the race?"

"You're in luck if you can stay for a couple-ah weeks. The ceremonial start is on the edge of town, the second Saturday in March. There are sometimes over a hundred mushers, so we start one every two minutes, and spotters at the twenty-six checkpoints keep track of their times.

"And the mushers have to take three rest stops at the checkpoints along the way. The first is for twenty-four hours, and the next two are for eight each."

"Mushers must be smart. They want to finish as fast as possible, but they can't go nonstop between the mandatory breaks, so they have to plan when to mush and when to race. Can they bring laptops and cell phones?"

"Nope, we want to keep the set-up authentic, but they can bring a regular watch. And they load the sled with enough supplies to get them to the checkpoints where they've stored stuff. Food for the huskies is the most important.

"And I'm playing a part this year. I'm the guy who'll radio storm conditions to the checkpoint spotters. But I've got it easier than the mushers. I go on a fully enclosed Alaskan-designed snowmobile that keeps the cold and snow out."

Electra had absorbed enough information to devise her own plan.

I've got something I'll trade with Miki if he'll let us watch the race with him. I'll tell him as soon as I can break in.

She did that at Miki's next word-stop.

"No wonder the Iditarod is so popular. We'd love to watch it if you'd let us be spectators with you. And I've got something that'd help you radio information to the checkpoints. It's a laptop containing my own Storm and Earthquake Tracker apps that are better than anyone's." Miki slapped the table before saying,

"Then you're smarter than anyone. We've got ourselves a deal. You and your team come back tomorrow, and me and Lusa will get it all worked out."

Renee got in the last question directed at Lusa. "Would you take us for a Reindeer-Dog lunch?"

"Sure. I think you'll like the seasoned blend of caribou, reindeer, beef, and pork. Vendors usually pile on glazed onions, ketchup, and mustard plus fries. They taste a bit stronger than what you get back home, but they're plenty safe."

Alonzo got in the last words. "And I'll pick up the tab."

Chapter 19

February 2173

"The Race for Survival"

Next morning, Electra added to the "brainy" status Miki had awarded her as soon as she explained the GUI's she was scrolling on his laptop.

Seismic Shock Predictor
Input: Big Data _____Proprietary Data _____
GPS Location ______Depth _Radius _
Minimum Intensity Level: ____
Date/Time Interval: Start ____ End ___

Relative Probability Density Function

Relative Probability

Time Axis

Relative Probability: _
(Equals RPDF integrated between Start and End)
Note: Seismic Levels: Light (4-4.9) Moderate (5-5.9) Strong (6-6.9) Major (7-7.9)

Severe Storm Forecaster
Input: Big Data _____Proprietary Data _____
GPS Location ______Storm Cell Radius ____
Minimum Level: ____
Date/Time Interval: Start ____ End ___
Atmospheric Parameters used: Temperature Pressure Humidity
Wind Speed Rotational Velocity
Vertical Wind Shear Electric Potential Diff.

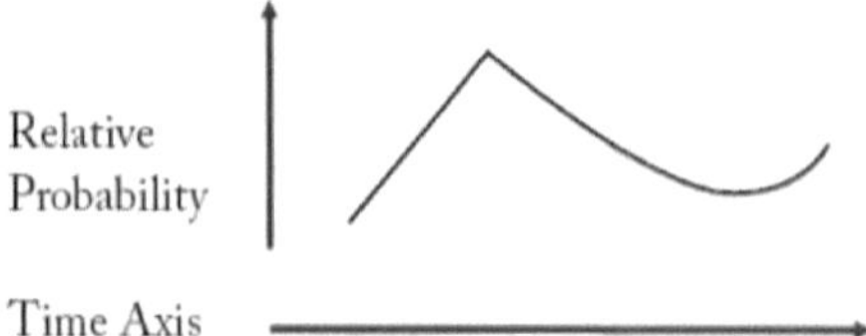

Relative Probability: ______
(Equals RPDF integrated between Start and End)
Note: Storm Levels: 1(75 mph) to 5(160+ mph)

"By contacting via the Internet my ace software developer, I have now downloaded onto your laptop my proprietary apps that will track and predict earthquakes and storms. We'll take it with us as we track the race by zooming along on snowmobiles. By the time we reach the finish line, you'll know everything I can teach you about using them."

"When do we start?" "Right now."

"OK, and while you're teaching me, Lusa will teach Renee all about Anchorage and Alaska by going to some tourist attractions. Tell-er where you'll take-er."

"Today we'll do the Anchorage Museum at Rasmussen Center first. It's a short walk from here and the weather's good. Then we'll take a taxi or sled ride to the Alaska Aviation Museum. It's only three miles, but you haven't been here long enough for Alaskan chill pills to do you much good. You can choose when we're ready to go."

Having heard enough from Lusa, Miki said, "Go now and let Electra start teaching."

While she did that, Alonzo confirmed the meetings in Juneau with the state agencies most interested in NAIA assistance.

The next two days repeated the routine, but on the third, Alonzo flew to Juneau and Miki took Electra on a chopper ride along the race route. She didn't need him to talk because she had already heard enough from watching videos. All she wanted was to let her senses experience as much of the route as flight time would allow.

What a magnificently sparkling landscape dotted with stands of trees on a cloudless day. It looks like snow machines aren't needed this year. And the trail winds across slopes, berms, and lakes, framed against mountains or steaming volcanoes. I'm glad the trail stays away from Mount Spurr, the big one near Anchorage, but some of the others look ready to glow. Might they blow during the race? My seismic tracker will know.

Electra noticed a brown-orange tinge on some of the frozen rivers.

Could that be manmade or natural pollution? Or maybe acidic chemicals coming from lava? I'd like to come back in the summer to study the ecology, but winter's the best season to hunt for dinosaur fossils. Denali National Park is a gold mine for digging them out. Maybe Plannert's got some bright young researcher studying how Dinos survived the cold. That's a topic for another trip.

By the time everyone reconvened the next day, Miki had the agenda set until race festivities.

"Everybody's on their own till next Thursday's pre-race banquet. We meet here a 6:30 so we can get there all together. And please dress warm and casual, Alaskan style."

Miki and Lusa led their three guests to the bar, buying them drinks before a senior Committee member waved for him to join a group of race officials clustered in front of a camera crew. Lusa took a meandering route to Miki's five-setting circular table, giving all three up close sights and sounds of the crowd. After all four sat, Alonzo asked Electra what she thought of the gathering.

She spoke just loud enough to be heard over the din.

"This beats all the Washington banquets I've attended. I've never seen so many straight-talking rugged men looking like they respect one another." She had more to say but couldn't. Miki and the camera crew were coming toward her, so she stood and moved toward him. Miki stopped in front, then turned sideways to introduce her to what had to be the leader of the crew.

"This is our NAIA Ambassador from DC. She's gonna help me keep track of the weather."

The leader, spotting an impromptu win-win-win opportunity, pulled Electra next to him before swinging to face the camera.

Years ago, Electra had mastered the art of interviewing from either side of the lens. She gave the interviewer crisp answers, using the right mix of words and body language that led him to additional questions she knew the audience would want answered, and she pulled Miki in for the last one.

"Ambassador Kittner's tracking software is the work of a genius. She's the smartest person from DC I've ever talked to."

The interviewer found some clever words to wrap up the interview. "Many critics would say they've never talked to even one. I hope you can do better than that."

Miki surprised him by replying.

"You just listen to what she tells me to say when we're on the Trail."

Electra could feel the collective excitement building, and as soon as the throaty sound of Miki's and Lusa's snowmobiles changed to an eager idle, Alonzo added his energetic words.

"I'll have a warmer seat, watching from the hotel, but you'll feel the thrill of the mushers from where you'll be sitting."

"I'll be safe tucked behind Miki, and ditto for Renee with Lusa. I know you'll be busy enough watching and pushing ahead on the NAIA, but time'll fly by even faster for us as soon as the sleds move out and we charge ahead with them."

Alonzo plugged in a crazy verse that had been featured all last week in a radio commercial.

"And if your tracking keeps the weather as good as today's, Miki can comb his dome while speeding to Nome and not get any flakes on his shoulders. Now go enjoy the race and stay healthy and safe." Alonzo felt a tinge of remorse as he watched the snowmobiles roar away, but it too faded because he knew his cyber-leg might not survive a mishap many miles from help. He felt even more grateful when he nestled into a comfy chair close to his room's TV.

Electra could hear the excited barking of sled dogs, even though she was a quarter mile from the start. Miki told his team it would last at least two hours because this year there were over sixty mushers. Miki's snowmobiles zoomed away an hour later, giving their passengers a thrill to remember. They stopped periodically to watch the dogs charge by, their barking now replaced by heavy panting but their drive undiminished, and Miki used the time to radio Electra's weather-tracking report to Race Control. Miki called a halt for a meal and rest at a checkpoint they reached soon after sunset, and had them back on the trail four hours later.

He repeated the pattern each day, staying close to the leaders. Electra expected the number of spectator snowmobiles would decline until they reached the halfway point and then start building, but it kept declining after that. Electra knew why. Both storm and seismic trackers reported bad news ahead.

During their last stop on the fourth day, Electra ran her trackers for an hour before telling Miki what to say.

"I'm seeing heavy winds building ahead from the northwest converging with heavier snow from the northeast. It's clear behind us for about fifteen miles, but then more wind and snow's closing in. There's an 85 percent probability this will last for the next three days, along with 75 percent for getting worse."

Miki rubbed his chin while saying, "We'll be heading through some forests; that might give us a wind break. What about your earthquake tracker?"

"Not much activity now, but there's an 80 percent probability it'll increase in two days, and it stays high even when I increase the intensity level."

Miki made the call before radioing in.

"This is more than I can say. You better tell Race Control."

Electra did that for the next four days, reporting worsening conditions that eliminated all but the heartiest spectators.

Just before they started in the darkness on the ninth day, a hopeful Miki said the leaders might reach Nome today or tomorrow, but Electra wasn't so sure.

"There's a 95 percent probability we'll run into a full-blown blizzard with wind gusts up to 75 mph. You connect us to Race Control and I'll tell them."

"OK, and so far, they've told me you're spot on. They want you to keep doin it."

"I wish I could control the weather, but my apps can't do that."

"Maybe not now, but your brain might do it someday if you keep doin it too."

The Sun might have been rising higher, but the intensity of the blizzard kept rising too, leading to whiteout conditions that forced Miki to halt when his instinctive experience told him. Only Electra and Lusa gathered with him when he did so, and he had to scream to keep the winds from whipping his words away.

"Check your trackers. We'll be crossing a frozen lake in a couple a—" Miki's words froze in his throat; hurricane-force gusts barrel-rolled a sled minus dogs and musher past them.

Electra shouted back,

"Storm intensity stays where it is, but seismic probability and intensity are going up."

Lusa yelled,

"We'll freeze if we don't keep moving." Miki yelled back,

"Get back in a keep close behind."

The gusts might have dropped to gale force, but the twisting trail across rutted terrain made it impossible for Electra to tell the difference, adding to her whiteout disorientation.

And then, a gigantic ground tremor broke through all of that. A crack split Miki's path; the two sides rushed apart faster than he could react. His snowmobile tumbled to the left. Electra saw Lusa's tumble into the fissure, taking its two riders with it, just before Miki's trapped its riders underneath.

Digging feverishly, Electra pulled herself out minutes later and then scrambled to the other side to help Miki. Then they stumbled to the gaping fissure, saying nothing until peering into it long enough for Miki to yell.

"Their snowmobile's upside down and thirty feet below. Lusa and Renee must be stuck underneath. Let's get a rope so you can climb down while I hold tight up here."

Electra ran back and dug out the equipment bag. She brought it to Miki, who knew what to do. He tied it around Electra's waist and then pointed for her to descend. The lightning brain elevated as soon as she went over the edge.

Get with it, soldier... I'm being dropped into a life-or-death situation...it's happened before...

A burst of lightning-like energy surged through Electra.

And I know what to do.

Moving with the speed of a seasoned Navy SEAL, she spotted Lusa first. She seemed uninjured and alert, so Electra tied her to the rope and jerked it for Miki to haul away. Lusa swung out and started moving up, but hung there. Miki's words echoed down.

"She's too much of a load. I need help."

Electra used her catlike agility and every ounce of strength to climb out, then doubled over just long enough for her muscles to replenish most of what she had used up. Then she gave a command to Miki. "Move closer to the edge and give me your end. That'll give me more leverage."

Miki did so, and they pulled as one with the strength of two, force multiplied by urgency. Lusa crawled out minutes later.

The trio worked as a silent, well-oiled team machine. Electra roped down; Miki and Lusa gripped from above. Electra went beyond the point where she found Lusa to find a comatose Renee. Electra's triage training kicked in.

She's breathing...legs and body free and clear and nothing seems broken...looks like the left shoulder's dislocated... uh-oh, the right arm's broken in two places...feels like the bone's sticking out underneath her parka...nothing we can do until we pull her out.

Electra gave two tugs. Renee swung out and began moving up. Electra followed.

When everyone was back together, Miki made the call.

"She'll lose her arm and maybe more if we don't get her to Nome. Lusa, help me flip my snowmobile so we can check it out. Electra, tie Renee's right arm to her body and wrap her in the blanket.

He yelled again fifteen minutes later; the wind still howled, but now the snowmobile was ready to do the same.

"After I get in, tie Renee to me. You two stay here. Call Race Control if you can get the radio workin and tell-em our predicament. We'll come get you as soon as we can. Lusa knows how to survive out here, so get with it."

Miki disappeared into the blizzard, which swallowed the snowmobile and all their hopes as he raced for their collective survival.

Electra followed Lusa's instructions. They couldn't make a windbreak for a fire, so they downed a couple of energy bars and had begun burrowing into the snow when Lusa shouted,

"Too bad the blanket's gone. We'll just have to hug close together." Electra yelled back.

"I can rope down and get the one in your snowmobile. Then you can pull me up."

Thirty minutes later, they were wrapped and tucked underneath the snow. Lusa gripped the flashlight and was peering at her watch when Electra wiggled to get her attention.

"I'm getting warmer. How long until someone rescues us?"

"Too bad we couldn't get the radio working. Miki has to get all the way to Nome. What with the blizzard, that could take at least six hours there and then six hours back. But I've been stuck before, so don't worry, we'll survive."

The girls had burrowed deep enough to insulate themselves from the dim light and raging wind. It also eliminated the noise, letting them doze fitfully until Electra felt a steadily growing vibration and told Lusa they should pop to the surface.

And when they did, the glare of approaching headlights cut through the storm. They scrabbled to their feet and waved. Two snow-cat ambulances stopped five yards in front.

Miki jumped out first and ran to them, carrying a flashlight. Lusa spoke first while glancing at her watch.

"How did you get her so fast?"

"Nome figured the blizzard'd trigger something, so they sent three snow-cats down the trail way before we crashed. We loaded Renee into one soon as we met and headed for you two. So here we are. And you look like you survived just fine."

Miki grabbed both of them in one giant bear hug. Electra spoke as soon as he let go.

"What about Renee?"

One of the medical techs answered.

"You did a good job wrapping her. It kept the open fracture from getting worse. That and the frigid temps helped keep her from bleeding out. The last report told us the emergency surgery saved her arm. She'll be in ICU for a couple of days, and after that, when she goes home, she'll need more work on the rods and screws that had to be inserted."

Electra saw Lusa's grimace when she said,

"Renee told me she likes to play volleyball. You think she can after awhile?"

"It all depends on the therapy and her will to get back to normal. She doesn't look like an Alaskan. Where's she from?

The ice-cold wind had blown Electra's tears away by the time she was ready to say,

"Brazil by way of DC. And please leave it to me. I'll do my best to get her back to normal."

Miki had heard enough from everyone and yelled,

"Let's get back in the cats and head to Nome. Tonight, that'll feel almost as good as goin home."

Chapter 20
April 2173

"More Problems Waiting"

Electra relied on Alonzo to make all travel arrangements as well as schedule initial therapy back in Los Angeles, and he exceeded her expectations. He even hired ambulances to transport all three to airports plus to and Electra's townhome.

Renee stayed there only one night. Alonzo and Electra took her the next day for a physical and psychological evaluation at a trauma and physical therapy center where she would stay during treatment.

Electra already knew from her life coach training what the counselor might say and made her own psychological assessment ahead of time, but she only listened to the therapist as he explained to Renee and her current caregivers his team's initial assessment. "Given the remote location and serious nature of Renee's injuries, you and Mr. Cortez have acquitted yourselves nicely, but now it's time for the professionals to intervene. They will begin physical therapy tomorrow, and depending on how well she responds, additional operations might be called for.

"It is common in these situations for the patient to experience periods of depression followed by anger at you for having indirectly caused the accident by putting her at risk. And we must abide by what she says because she is an adult.

"She tells me she lives with a Mr. Noah Hansen when not staying with you. Is that correct?"

Electra nodded.

"Renee wants him to be her ombudsman while hospitalized, and she prefers living with him full-time when discharged. Would you please bring him with you for our follow-up meeting tomorrow afternoon?"

"Of course."

"That is all for today. Please come back at 2 p.m."

Renee's combination of splint and sling eliminated hugs, and her glower told both Electra and Alonzo she didn't want to hear from them, so they left after thanking the therapist.

Electra stared out the window while Alonzo drove, but she turned her head when he began speaking.

"I've seen abrupt mood changes when some of my SEAL teamers got injured. And you can use me as an example. You saw how PTSD affected me. I think I'll bring that up tomorrow. Maybe he'll treat her for that too."

"Please do. I had forgotten all about it. And that reminds me. I'll call Noah and tell him to meet us there tomorrow."

"No, I have a better idea. He works for you at your consulting office, doesn't he? So, let's pick him up for lunch. You can give him the lowdown."

Electra smiled for the first time since landing in LA.

"I think I better set up a partner's office for you in LA."

"OK, but you'll always be my boss, except when Monet's with us..." Electra didn't want to talk with Eve and Nari until after briefing Noah, so she told him to meet them at the curb. Alonzo drove while she handled the usual greetings and changed the topic after Alonzo placed the pizza order.

"Renee broke her arm when her snowmobile toppled into a crevasse during a blizzard. We dug her out and rushed her to Nome for emergency surgery that saved her arm, but she won't be back to work any time soon.

"She'll be hospitalized during therapy, which starts today. While there, she wants you to be her ombudsman, and when released, wants to live with you full-time. It's a big responsibility and completely up to you. That's why the therapist asked you to join us this afternoon. Have you ever been a caregiver?"

Noah didn't hesitate.

"No, but I took care of lots of pets when I was a kid. How's she feeling?"

Electra nodded at Alonzo to bring him in.

"Depressed and angry. I've seen the effects of PTSD. Hey, here come the pizza slices. Let's let the shrink tell you more."

Noah kissed Renee and sat next to her as soon they entered the conference room. Electra sat opposite, with Alonzo to her left and the therapist to her right. He started the session as soon as Noah and Renee looked ready.

"I'm pleased you're here, and it looks like Renee is too. I imagine Electra and Alonzo gave you enough background info, but is there anything else you would like to know?"

"No, sir. Renee will fill in any missing pieces." "Good. Well then, please tell us your intentions." "I-uh want to marry her when the time's right."

Noah didn't know what else to say, but the therapist did. "Please tell us more…"

After twenty minutes of listening to Noah and Renee list their plans, the therapist looked like he had heard enough.

"You be a fine companion. Why don't you go with Renee while I wrap up with your friends?"

Noah looked relieved during the drive to the office, and his words showed it whenever Electra asked him to comment when they met with the others once inside. He and Kai continued in Kai's cubicle; Alonzo and Electra did the same with Eve and Nari in their office.

Alonzo didn't flinch when Nari handed him Elton, and he was actually cooing to him when Eve began talking.

"This is the very first time Elton gets to see his godmother and godfather at the same time. Nari and I thought you'd be the best person to hold that title, so you'll have to visit often enough to give him a solid male role model."

Electra used Eve's words to segue in.

"And it's never too soon to give him a solid school foundation. Even though he's only five months old, we should enroll him in a magnet school system's daycare program for gifted children. That way he's already in, and Nari doesn't have to worry about quotas and qualifying exams when he moves into grade school and beyond." Nari asked, "You know of any?"

"I'll research for them, and we can enroll him in a couple of weeks." Eve ended the discussion.

"Electra's a gifted researcher. We'll take her pick."

Alonzo and Electra departed soon afterward for her townhome, and that evening, while he was talking to Monet, she decided to call Marne, who sounded pleased to hear from her life coach as soon as she recognized Electra's voice.

"Troy told me you had to cancel his first session, something about you going on a trip, and I knew you'd call me when you got back. Why don't the three of us have dinner at my place?"

"No, I feel obliged to give him his first session before then, so why don't I do that first and you and I can have dinner soon after?"

"I like that. Do you know when it'll be?"

"No. I'll call him after we end ours and let you know as soon as he picks the date, time, and location."

"I know he'll pick his condo. Be sure he's on his best behavior."

"I will. Some of my life coaching tools keep me tuned in. Bye-bye." Troy's manners looked as good as he did when she started the evening session in his study a week later.

"I have a couple of handouts for you to study between now and next time. Each covers a topic many Hollywood types want to explore. Here's the first."

THE IMPOSTER SYNDROME

People who struggle with imposter syndrome believe that they are undeserving of their achievements and the high esteem in which they are, in fact, generally held. They feel that they aren't as competent or intelligent as others might think—and that soon enough, people will discover the truth about them.

POTENTIAL CAUSES

- Pushing too hard for "Perfection"
- Comparing yourself to only "High Achievers"
- Wanting to be only a "Superhero"
- Shunning all "Help"
- Needing to "Learn It All"

Electra gave him only a second to glance at it before saying, "Between now and our next session, I want you to rank-order their importance for you and include a brief explanation why.

"And here's the second."

DEALING WITH TRAUMA

People tend to bury the episodes of trauma they have experienced.

TWO TYPES

- External: Anyone can see the results
  Example: Domestic Violence
- Internal: Seen or felt only by the Individual
  Example: Anger for No Job Promotion

Address it with the ECHO Model

- Events: Identify major episodes
- Context: Articulate the setting
- Homeostatic Shifts: Changes made
- Outcomes: Resultant Behaviors and Feels

Combination of Events and Contexts determine what outcomes satisfy these three Needs: Physiological Safety Love

Electra waited for Troy's reaction, which came with a troubled look. "I need your help doing this between now and next time. How do I?"

"Use the Trauma sheet when doing the rank-ordering." Troy looked satisfied with the answer, so Electra said,

"Now, please tell me what problems you've been working on." Ninety minutes later, Electra ended the session.

"that's plenty for tonight. Please call me when you're ready to reconvene."

"I will. And I don't owe you anything for tonight?"

"No, but my normal rate applies in the future. I'm certain you'll get your money's worth."

"I know I will. Let me walk you to your car." "Thanks, but the door will be fine."

Now that the current crop of problems had been resolved or at least put into remission, Electra could return to two of her most favorite management practices: "Management by Walking About," and "If it Ain't Broke Don't Fix it."

Each day while in the office, she would observe her people but not intrude unless they asked for her thoughts. And her successful style had earned their respect long ago.

Every good manager knows what his people are doing, so when Alonzo told her he needed to return to Washington, she understood and offered suggestions he might like.

"Please be sure to tell China about our Alaskan adventure. You should also let Feather and Chaska know about the progress you made on our NAIA and IPWA agendas. And call me when you have scoped out our International Ambassador Trip agenda."

"Will do; anything else?"

"Just a big thank you to my number one partner. Travel safe." Alonzo did, and it showed when meeting with China the day after returning.

"You look full of energy. Tell me about Alaska."

China listened for a half hour. When Alonzo finished, she said,

"I watched a local news clip showing an interview taken at the Iditarod pre-race banquet. I didn't see you, but I did see Electra, and it sounds like her storm and earthquake trackers work better than anyone's."

"And she left copies on Miki's laptop. That'll earn us extra credit for another visit."

"When will that be?"

"Electra and Miki will figure that out. I'm busy with things…"

Zoltan Sultani, like Alonzo, was always busy but still found time to track an elusive but nonetheless intriguing target, Electra Kirchner.

He had seen the Iditarod interview and from it, devised the solution to a festering problem, which he shared only with himself.

I no longer have to chase her down. I know an easier way to get what I want, and as soon as I do, my techies can fit it into my plans that will stun Mother Nature and the world. How nice for me and Bigger Bro.

Chapter 21
May 2173

"The Ambassadors on the Road"

Troy looked upset when he ushered Electra into his study for this evening's Life Coaching session, so Electra spoke like any competent coach would.

"Please tell me about your latest problem."

"I was having an after-dinner drink with some of my actor friends when the topic of intelligence came up. One of the ladies challenged me to solve this puzzle.

"Pretend I'm living in the Land of Liars. Everyone there always tells either the truth or lies, and you don't know which group a stranger falls in. Liars live in the Fibbing Village, and the others in Truth Town. I'm a truth-teller, walking on a road I've never been on before, and I come to a fork in the road manned by a guard who knows which path leads to Fibbing Village or Truth Town, and he'll answer my question, but I don't know which group he belongs to. "So, here's the puzzle. What question do I ask so I know which way to go? I couldn't figure it out, and I couldn't understand her answer. Maybe you can."

Electra thought for only a second before answering.

"Ask him to point to the road he would take to go home." Then she waited for his reaction.

"That's what she said, but why does it work?"

"There's a whole set of brain teasers like this that rely on an omniscient point of view. Suppose he's a liar. Then he'll point to the truth-teller's path. And if he's a truth-teller, he'll point the same way. Does that clear things up?"

"It's clearer, but my brain's not as sharp as it used to be. Can your Life Coaching boost my I.Q.?"

"I think so. It's fifty percent determined by genes and fifty percent by what you do to keep your brain active. We've talked about some of them in previous sessions, but let me run through all of them before we focus today on I.Q. exercises."

"Could you write them down for me so it's easier to follow?"
"Sure, it'll take only a minute or two."

Troy gave her a pen and pad of paper. She handed them back when finished.

I.Q.-Boosting Activities.

1. Meditate.
2. Exercise.
3. Keep body weight low and fast occasionally.
4. Sleep just enough.
5. Read widely every day.
6. Work crossword puzzles, Sudoku, and word jumbles; play Scrabble, Chess, Othello, and Go; write poetry.
7. Expose yourself to new experiences that broaden your mindset and increase your points of view. Mindset: your set of beliefs, attitudes, ethics, and approach to relationships. It's a generalization of the Myers-Briggs personality assessment. M-B Dimensions: Where you get your Energy (Extrovert/Introvert); How you gather information (Sensing/Intuition); How you make decisions (Thinking/Feelings); How you deal with the outside world (Judging/Perceiving)
8. Practice new skills.
9. Socialize. Relations will build cognitive and emotional intelligence as well as generate brain-stimulating hormones.
10. Consider taking brain-boosting supplements, electrical stimulation, or stem cell injections.
11. Learn a new language.
12. Play a musical instrument.

"Eleven of these recommendations are environmental factors that will help you build a cognitive brain reserve containing more brain cells and interneural connections. Guess which one isn't."

Troy scanned the list before pointing to the tenth. "How do I get electrical stimulation?"

"If a medical technician has already installed a UMPP in you—that's an acronym for Universal Multi-Parallel Port—we can plug a cable from my laptop into it. Or you can wear an electro-stimulation brain cap that has a cable I plug in."

"What about stem cell injections?"

"A doctor withdraws stem cells from your bone marrow, modifies them to attach to brain cells, and then injects them into your blood." Troy's scrunched nose agreed with his words.

"I don't like pain. Let's talk about number seven."

"We'll do better than that. You can take a Myer-Briggs evaluation test online right now."

Electra let Troy end the session an hour later after she turned off her laptop.

"Now I know why you turn me on. I'm ENFP and you're ISTJ. Aren't opposites supposed to attract? Maybe we can do some stimulating exercises together."

Electra didn't like the body language that came with his words, but she maintained a professional demeanor.

"That would be inappropriate for a consultant-client relationship. Call me when you're ready to schedule another session, and until then, practice some of the first five."

Troy followed her to the front door.

Electra could put away any thoughts about Troy until he called for another session, so she directed most of her attention to the people in the consulting office. She didn't intrude because everyone seemed happily busy, but she followed Renee's recovery by treating Noah to lunch enough times to realize Renee didn't want to see her.

However, when Alonzo called two days later, she knew he wanted to see her soon.

"When I explained more to Monet about our ambassador's role, she says she can handle it for Africa and you and me can take it to India. That means we get Sanjay to set up a trip to the indigenous people and places to visit. I sent him an Email telling what the IPWA is all about, and he shot one back a day later. And guess what?"

"Please tell me."

"Maybe you've been talking to Eve and she's been talking to Nila, but he knows all about it, and he used his political connections to get buy-in. He says he'll come along with us. All he needs from us is an arrival date in Mumbai. We can stay with him and Nila before leaving a couple a days later; so, when do you want to leave?"

"I assume I'll fly to DC and travel with you." "That's it."

"Timing's everything, and you called at a time when my calendar's uncluttered. You decide."

"I pick leaving on Saturday, the fifteenth. With the five-thousand-mile distance and Mumbai's clock ten-and-a-half hours ahead of DC's, we can get over the jet lag disorientation and still be on the road by Tuesday."

"I hope we won't be driving. India's road and highway system is better than twenty years ago, but for us, it won't easily get to the right places and people. We better let Sanjay pick the places and the best means of transportation."

"I'll let him know. And I'll Email you your boarding pass info for your flight to DC. I'll meet you at the gate. And like we did for Alaska, don't pack anything. We'll let Nila and Sanjay shop for us."

"I feel like I should say 'OK Boss'."

"Go right ahead, but I know who's really in charge. See you in a week."

Electra spent most of the time until her DC flight retrieving information from her lightning brain about previous visits to India made in previous lifetimes, which only she knew about. She also searched online for current facts. By the time she and Alonzo arrived in Mumbai, she knew as much as Sanjay and Nila combined but kept it to herself.

Nila and Sanjay treated their guests with traditional Indian hospitality. They used the customary namaste greeting that signifies courtesy and respect, and let Electra decide when to talk about business. And when she did, she let Sanjay run the meeting.

He began by summarizing enough about indigenous tribes.

"We have over 700 ethnic groups that make up about ten percent of the population, but I picked five places to visit where I have contacts who can get the word out to the dominant tribes—the Gonds in Central India, the Bhils in Western, and the Santals of Eastern. Here's a sketch of where we'll go to meet them and others."

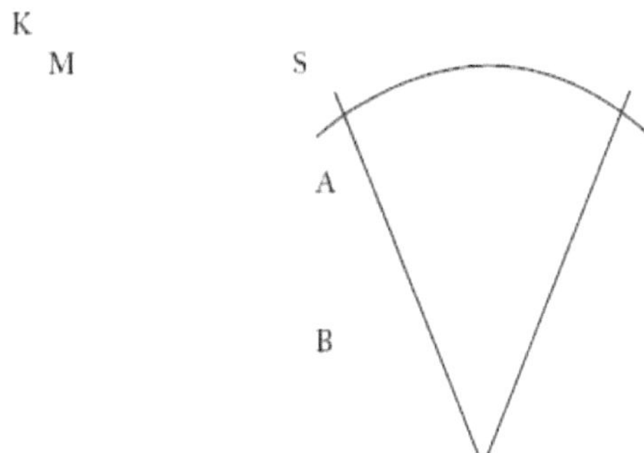

"We start in Mumbai, then go to Kanpur, followed by Sirakulam and Bangalore, then up to Antapur before returning to Mumbai."

Alonzo asked the obvious question. "How are we getting to all these places?"

"By train. Our roads and hi-ways are much better than thirty years ago, but they're still not up to your standards for reaching the places you need to see."

Electra knew the answer to the next question he would ask, but preferred to listen to Sanjay's answer after he asked it.

"What do you expect us to see."

"A teeming, well-educated, and young population stuck in a climate threatened by too much heat and humidity plus more tropical cyclones dumping too much rain. They hope this IPWA can speak for them and get action."

Electra decided to say,

"That's what it's supposed to do. I think we've reviewed enough. Let's let your contacts fill in the rest…"

Sanjay's contacts were as good as advertised. Every single one liked what the IPWA offered and knew even more than Sanjay about threats to the environment. By the time they reached the final stop, Electra no longer needed to take notes but simply listened.

His Antapur contact, a thoroughly modern and youthful-thinking woman wearing a saree, spoke pleasantly yet authoritatively.

"Like everywhere else, climate change is real and present in varied forms, but you might not realize that droughts, landslides, and earthquakes add to our biodiversity loss and continue destroying natural surroundings and habitats so vital to our indigenous people. And occasionally, they create hotspots for breeding zoonotic diseases. The Indian government promises to do more, but they haven't delivered enough. Please tell me more about what you offer." Electra started, but she let Sanjay and Alonzo finish the pitch. As he was about to speak, Alonzo's look of concern while Sanjay drove to the station touched Electra, making her feel obligated to tell the truth.

"I must have picked up a bug yesterday. I have a headache and chills. Sanjay, do you have anything I can take?"

"It could be caused by all the stress you've been under, but I'll stop along the way and pick something up. And all of us can rest on the train."

Alonzo's tone matched his words.

"Fat chance doing that. Even though you bought us compartments, all the trains have standing room only."

Electra defused what might have become an argument by saying, "I'll think restful thoughts."

Electra felt good enough a couple of days after returning to LA later to return multiple unanswered calls Troy had left, and decided afterward Alisha would drive rather than let him come get her for a "stimulating" dinner he would cook at his condominium that evening. Alisha did most of the talking en route.

"My driving reduces the time I'll be with him and gives me a quick exit if he becomes too motivated. But please stay with me if he gets out of hand."

"I will, and I know you'll let him down empathetically. But don't be too nice like you often are. Don't let him push you around…"

Alisha didn't like the hungry look in Troy's eyes when he opened the door.

"You look good enough to eat. Why don't we—" Electra tried to redirect his intentions from her body to his mind with her words. "Tonight, we can talk about creative wellness. It's holistic, which means it comprises mental, emotional, spiritual, physical, social, environmental, and financial factors. Why don't we—" Troy's lips pressing against hers stifled any further words.

His hands started moving in the direction only he liked. His left started rubbing harder and faster toward the spot on her body he liked the best while he used his right and shorter but heavier body to pin her to the entryway wall. She didn't like what she was seeing in the mirror hanging above the table and lamp on the opposite wall; she pushed him away when his fingers groped too far.

"Please stop. I came back with some sort of zoonotic virus and it might not be safe for you." Troy pulled her back and then started yelling.

"You always give me excuses. I'm tired of waiting, so now I'll take what I want." Troy grabbed her by the shoulders before pivoting and throwing her toward the table while ripping off her blouse. Electra kept from falling, but the lamp and mirror crashed to the hardwood floor, making a noise that added to his incoherent words.

Electra's lightning brain took command, and this time it unleashed her Monster from the Id. She kneed him in his privates and then threw him against the entry door. He bounced toward her but managed to land a solid right that split her lower lip. The taste of her own blood excited her. She lusted for his.

She punched him in the throat, which stood him up, then used a SEAL throw to put him on his back before leaping on top. She was about to shower him with blows, but without warning, the Monster submerged into the lightning brain's nether world. Electra collapsed in a shower of tears.

Pounding on the door accompanied by a loud masculine voice brought her back.

"This is the Police. Open up."

Electra rose before Troy and did so. A young officer flashed a badge and bolted in.

Troy stuttered, "Sh-she attacked me. Arrest her."

The officer's partner, a young female, begged to differ.

"Be quiet. That's not what it looks like. I'll get your story and my partner will get hers. Come with me."

Electra and the male officer remained in place after she led him to another room. Then he did likewise, examining Electra closely before speaking.

"I've seen your face before. Even with all the blood, you look like that Hollywood Life Coach, Electra-Alisha Kirchner. Is that you?" Speaking clearly and showing little emotion, Electra knew how to handle the situation.

"I am, and my client, Troy Shandell, scheduled a coaching session for this evening right here. As you can see, I'm not damaged too badly, so I prefer not to press charges."

"Let me get your full story. Then me and my partner will decide what to do."

Electra drove away two hours later, maintaining an unblemished record, and thanks to Alisha, Troy received only a warning to avoid further episodes of domestic violence. He promised to do so by finding a different Life Coach. The current one had taught him enough.

Electra invented a cover for the split lip which satisfied everyone, but she needed to tell the truth to Marne, whom she called two days later. Marne gasped several times but said nothing until Electra asked for her thoughts.

"You taught me that no matter how well I think I know someone, there's always stuff hidden deep inside that I'll never know about until it breaks out. I guess that's what happened. We're still friends, aren't we?"

"Sure, and he's reminded me why I like females better than males, no matter the type of love I'm looking for."

"Well then, why don't you come for brunch next Sunday? I'll cook up something we'll both like."

"I'm feeling better already. What should I bring?" "Just you and Alisha."

"Now that's something I know all about. See you then."

Chapter 22
June 2173

"Fare Thee Well"

Marne sat perfectly still, waiting for Electra to finish before giving her opinion.

"I know how you feel. Renee doesn't really hate or blame you for the accident. And unlike what my son used to do, she didn't throw a tantrum or slam doors in your face. His words hurt, but I didn't let them bother me for too long. We joke about it now and then." "Maybe I can do that with her, but it will be just for the two of us. Noah doesn't need to be part of this."

"Maybe when she takes you out for a Mother's Day tribute. When my son takes me out for a Mother's Day brunch, he always says something like I'm the best Mom in the whole world. I know he's exaggerating, but the way he looks at me when he says it tells me how much he means it, and that means the world to me."

"Then I'll stay the course. I won't push the issue; I'll let time speak to her."

"And if it goes on too long, just tell me and I'll speak to her."

Electra kept following her own advice while keeping engaged in all her projects. When Alonzo called a week later, he asked about Renee after they had discussed business. Electra spoke for a couple of minutes; then he said,

"As far as I know, neither Nari nor Eve ever yelled at Su-Lin, but they did say mean things about her to me and Nila. We just listened because we didn't want to incur Nari's wrath or Eve's stinging words. Su-Lin's patience and empathy got the better of them. She never showed her feelings, but the way they treated her must have occasionally hurt. You want me to talk to Renee?"

"Thanks, but no. I don't want her to think I'm using you to pressure her."

"OK, but let me know if you do."

Nothing occurred during the next weeks that disturbed the relative calm in Electra's professional or personal worlds. She followed her customary routine of taking Kai or Noah out for lunch on alternate weeks, letting them lead the discussion.

This week, Noah and his whimsical look sat across from her and spoke while eating dessert.

"Renee's coming around, and I'm doing my part by not saying anything about you. She's almost done with therapy, which means she'll be ready to come back to work with me and Kai unless she looks somewhere else."

Noah's pause left a space for Electra to speak.

"Has she regained mobility? Does it hurt if she moves her arm too far?"

"I think it does, but you know Renee. She doesn't show much emotion. Volleyball is out of the question, but we'll try the surfing stuff in about a month."

"Good. Please invite me sometime to watch your volleyball practice. Tell me, how's she treating you?"

Noah didn't hesitate talking to Electra about an intimate subject. "OK, but she's not as interested in sex as before. I'm not worried; we'll work it out..."

Unbeknownst to anyone other than Renee, she knew how to work things out. The home pregnancy test she had taken after missing her second period worried her, but she knew the reason. Whoever raped her had made her pregnant. Her baby bump hadn't become visible to anyone, and it never would.

Renee alibied to Noah she had errands to run on a Saturday afternoon that would take the place of watching his volleyball practice, this one spectated by Electra. After his teammates picked him up, she drove to an unadvertised location where she picked up items ordered a week ago on the Deep-Dark Web. And then she drove to the only place she knew no one would intrude; Electra's townhome.

Renee spread a blanket on the bathroom floor before taking two pills instead of one, guaranteed to cause contractions that would force an abortion. She waited for as long as her patience allowed, but when nothing stirred, she took another before using a modified coat hanger to coax Mother Nature.

But the delayed reaction to the overdose triggered more than Renee could handle. The cramping doubled her up, causing nausea leading to vomiting. The last she saw before passing out was blood gushing.

Electra didn't bother closing the front door when she entered her townhome after returning from the volleyball practice. Her instincts told her something was amiss. When she walked up the stairs, she distinctly remembered turning the bathroom light off.

But what she saw told her the cause, and it gagged her, bringing her to her knees next to a comatose Renee. The gruesome sight elevated Electra to her highest state.

This looks even worse than dear Robin's miscarriage two lifetimes ago… call 911…

The dispatcher's calm voice listened when Electra screamed, "Please, I need your help. My daughter's got a botched abortion. She's unconscious and blood's still pouring out."

"What's your name and her name?"

"I'm Electra Kirchner, and my daughter's Renee."

"I see your cell phone location. I'm sending an ambulance right now."

Electra did nothing after the call except remain close to Renee and whisper while her eyes hovered over Renee's.

"Renee, please come back… don't leave me this way..."

Somewhere in Renee's deepest reaches, the words roused her. Her eyes fluttered when she struggled to speak.

"Mu-Mother, I-I'm so sorry I made ah mess. I oh-only wanted you to be pr-proud of me. I-I ah-always lu-loved you."

Cradling Renee's head in her arms, Electra stammered, "But-but why?"

"I-uh ra-rape… neh-neh-ver tell any—" Renee's violent thrashing came before a death rattle that Electra had heard in previous lifetimes.

Electra pulled her to her breast, her tears streaming onto Renee's cheeks, but Renee could not feel them. Her essence had vanished. Electra knew she would never return.

Gone… fare thee well my third daughter, now gone…first my clone child Airee…then brave little Qama from Lebanon…and now my Rainforest Girl. I thought I did all I could to keep them safe…they were mine but I didn't, or couldn't keep my promise…I thought my love could, but no, they weren't mine...they were only given to me for a brief moment in time…a time for me to cherish…I did all I could but it wasn't enough…

The ambulance med-techs pulled Electra off, hoping to find signs of life but couldn't. Electra answered all their questions as they put Renee on a stretcher. Electra insisted she stay next to her daughter for the somber ride to the closest hospital morgue.

And she did, crying silently all the way.

Chapter 23
July 2173

"The Search for Redemption"

Not even Eve could find consoling words to calm a screaming Noah when Electra let the office know the next day about Renee's death. Kai stared into the distance, avoiding everyone.

Electra expected those responses as well as the one coming from pragmatic Nari, but even she couldn't stifle all she felt.

"You better let Alonzo know right away. Maybe he'll say something useful."

Electra told everyone to go home. She wanted to be alone some place other than her townhome, where she could grieve privately while beginning her search for redemption. She called Alonzo late that afternoon. He said nothing until she had finished.

"Holy camoly, you must still be in shock. What might have triggered it?"

"I haven't a clue. I'll ask Noah when he settles down. Maybe he knows something."

"You want me to fly in for whatever remembrance service you'll set up?"

"No, you and I can hold our own when I visit."

"OK, let me know when you know. You want me to tell China?" "Please, and take care."

Electra asked Eve and Nari the next day if they would host a remembrance ceremony to honor Renee. Eve didn't hesitate to answer.

"Sure, and we'll keep it close. Just you, me, Nari, Noah and Kai, and any friends Noah wants to bring. What about Alonzo?"

"I already called him. We'll hold our own the next time I'm at his office."

Electra spoke last and least at the gathering Friday afternoon, preferring to listen to what Renee's closest friends said. Eve did her best to find helpful words when she spoke to each person individually while they nibbled on Nari's simple buffet.

Nari's final words to Electra before she left jolted her back to the here and now.

"You need to go someplace other than your townhome or this office. If I felt like you look, I'd work out of Alonzo's office and stay with China. You have to get yourself back together."

"You're right. Thanks for reminding me."

Alonzo guessed the reason for Electra's call the next day. When she said she'd like to visit, he took charge.

"I'll book your flight and then send you the info for printing your boarding pass. And I'll meet you at the gate when you deplane." "What date?"

"Leave that to me. You'll know when you print your pass."

Electra arrived late afternoon on Friday of the following week. Alonzo kept a constant stream of chatter going while driving to China's and promised to pick her up Saturday morning.

Electra used her key to open the front door and as expected, found a silent China waiting inside. She clutched both hands with hers as soon as Electra reached out, then led her to the kitchen.

After putting a minimal dinner on the table, she said,

"You don't look like you're eating enough, and that's not unusual after the trauma you've been through."

Electra rallied enough to say,

"I teach trauma management in my Life Coaching program. I guess I'm not a good role model."

"Alonzo and I will help snap you into a better mental state, and we won't rush it. Why don't you take your usual morning run before Alonzo picks you up tomorrow? It should help."

"Good idea. I'll take your advice."

The endorphins helped, but not enough to satisfy Alonzo, and he told her so while they snacked on muffins and doughnuts while sipping from cans of Coke.

"Now it's my turn to lecture you and draw a diagram. We've got to get you in a better mental state. Take a look at this."

Alonzo fashioned it in big, bold words before saying more.

BRAIN WAVE MENTAL STATES

MOST ACTIVE

- **Beta: Rational and Critical Thinking**
- **Alpha: Hypnotic-Like Absorbing Info Like Watching TV**
- **Theta: Borderline Creative Flitting Between It and Alpha Like taking a Shower**
- **Delta: Dream State when Asleep Subconscious Active**

LEAST ACTIVE

Your Challenge: Set Your Intentions for the Next Day as you Fall Asleep

"Do it tonight. Sunday, we can compare yours with mine. And to get us started, let me tell you what I've been following. Do you know about the East Coast Infrastructure problem?"

"No; sorry, my mind's been elsewhere. Please tell me."

"A number of key roads and bridges are sinking. Several inland, as well as along the Atlantic, have already collapsed. Maybe it's rising sea levels or low-intensity earthquakes. And coastal Europe is seeing the same. Let's watch some videos and then have dinner with Monet."

Monet's diplomatic bearing kept everyone from spiraling into painful emotions, and by the time Alonzo drove Electra home, she felt ready to take up Alonzo's challenge. He would pick her up Monday morning for them to continue.

Electra thought she had set her intentions to at least match Alonzo's level, but she knew she hadn't when he told her his.

"What if we contact your Professor Plannert? Let him recommend a bright young researcher we can leverage for studying more about East Coast subsidence. And if you regain your cleverness, perhaps you can find a link that NASA might like."

"You're beginning to sound like me. I like it. And my brain still remembers that this is a good time to call."

It was. Professor Plannert rose to greet them when they appeared two hours later at his office.

"I am happy to see you both, and I must say Alonzo looks strapping but Electra looks peaked. You never contacted me after your Alaskan adventure. Might you have picked up a virus?"

Alonzo covered by replying,

"That's my fault. I got sidetracked thinking about what your Committee might like to research, but it worked out for something better. We've come across an East Coast Infrastructure Subsidence problem?"

"Indeed, yes. One of our civil engineers raised the issue. She's not on the Committee, mind you, but she is very competent. In fact, she reports that one of her cohorts from New Jersey captured on video bolts of energy beaming down from the heavens and into the land beneath a suspected bridge she was studying. Unfortunately, the strike couldn't be corroborated, but I think you might like to talk with her. Would you like to come tour next meeting?"

This time, Electra spoke for herself.

"No, my schedule won't allow it, but Alonzo will contact her."

"Very well. I will Email you all the information he needs. And may I treat you to lunch?"

"Thank you but no. Alonzo and I have another place we need to go..."

Chapter 24

July 2173

"The NASA Conjecture"

Because he was driving, Alonzo asked Electra a perfectly normal question.

"You better tell me how to get to this another place we need to go."

"I don't know its location."

"But that's what you said to Plannert."

"I prevaricated. Diplomats and politicians do that all the time."

"Yes, and those are two roles you play so well. But you're doing that more and more when it's not necessary. What gives?"

Electra shifted her languishing gaze from the space in front of the car to the driver, her tone showing the same level of indifference. "I'm tired and losing interest. Humans are the most destructive species, always blocking whatever good intentions we might have." "That doesn't sound like the Electra I know. I sure hope you snap out of your funky mental state and come back to what you used to be. And don't give me your pat answer. You've used up your quota of perhapses."

Electra parried his words with some of hers.

"Perhaps you're right. Please take me home. I'll call you when I have more energy."

When Electra lingered in bed the next morning instead of rousing herself to greet the dawn, Alisha sensed Electra's downward spiral had worsened and said so.

"You really need to suit up for an endorphin-generating un. That will prepare you to dive into your high-priority tasks like you used to."

"No, I just don't feel like it today. I'm tired of pushing myself to do things or help others, or to kid myself about what a wonderful life we have, in which you and I are supposed to look for new opportunities that always lead to obstacles ready to trip us up." "Well, why don't you let me take over until you regain your step?" "No, I pre, uh, no, I don't want to."

"You're supposed to be our rational persona. I've never been able to change your thinking when you're like this. I think it's time for you to talk with Indira. I'll listen in while you do."

Electra did that two hours later. Indira spoke as soon as she saw Electra's disheveled appearance.

"Why don't you settle down, sit still, and let Alisha tell me what's bothering you?"

After five minutes, Alisha returned to the shadows, leaving Electra under the tutelage of Indira.

"Alisha, who is your empathetic and emotional persona, has already worked through grieving for Renee. It is time for you to do the same. And remember that grieving too long won't help you, and it never helps the dearly departed. You either move ahead or fall behind. No one can stand still in a world that is constantly changing."

Electra could feel her lightning brain begin to shift.

"I know you're right, but I can't seem to climb out of my depression. What should I do?"

"I won't give you all that you should, but I will get you started. Use it as a challenge to bring yourself back. I call it 'The NASA Conjecture.' And it begins with the Space-Based Power Grid I presented to you several years ago. Do you recall it?"

Electra could feel interneural connections responding to Indira's challenge.

"Isn't that a ring of solar-powered satellites that can beam bolts laser-like energy into our land-based electrical power grid?"

"Yes. Watch the monitor. I shall scroll the diagram you already have."

Indira gave Electra enough time to reacquaint herself with it before saying more.

"What might happen if the satellites are repositioned close together?"

More connections turned on, matching Electra's growing enthusiasm.

"We might have a gigantic weapon if we focus all the beams."

"Excellent. And now, I will give you one more clue, using the word that Alonzo says you shouldn't. Perhaps you can connect this to the East Coast Infrastructure Problem."

"I think I can, and I'll do this via NASA. But do you think I can make them pay attention?"

"I can do better than that. I know. Now all you need do is to continue thinking about what we have just covered so you are back to the Electra who exceeds mere mortals."

Indira's GUI disappeared. A reinvigorated Electra remained.

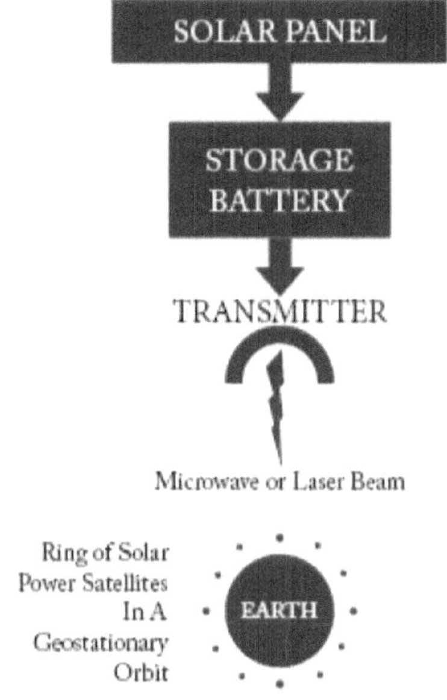

She surprised Alonzo the next morning by calling him right after finishing her dawn's early run.

"You sound full of energy. I guess you took my words to heart." "And to mind also. Please come get me. I know where we're going next."

At Alonzo's office two hours later, Electra said they should call Britt at NASA.

"I've come up with what we'll call the NASA Conjecture. It'll make connections between SBPG satellites and the East Coast Infrastructure problem. Do you recall what SBPG stands for?" Alonzo's look combined both surprise and delight that the old

Electra had returned.

"Space-Based Power Grid. And guess what? Britt Starling called me a couple of days ago. She says she's been leaving messages for you, but you haven't returned them, so she called me, thinking I'd know your whereabouts. I didn't tell you because you seemed so distracted."

"Well, I'm not now. Find out what she wants, and don't tell her anything about Renee. Just tell her I've been traveling."

"Should I call her now?"

"Of course. Follow the rule you already know—it's better to ask for forgiveness than seek permission. And you do all the talking; I'll listen from the shadows."

"OK, Boss. I'll do it now."

An hour later, Alonzo summarized the call.

"DOD's having control issues with its SBPG satellite ring. She wants us to meet with her and her team in Houston to help them figure out what's wrong. She didn't give me any more than that but will when we get here. I guess she's worried about my call to her being hacked. Anyway, I'm supposed to call her back when I know when we'll be there. When do you want to go?"

"I'm ready now. You set it up." "Yes, Boss. That's my job, Mon." "OK, Partner. Do it now."

Electra detected tension in the conference room as soon as she and Alonzo entered. She pretended otherwise but knew the cause. Though Britt and Boomer sat at both ends of the table, Zoltan Sultani sat in a chair against the wall, his bald head and gruff expression casting a pall.

Britt spoke while seated as soon as Electra and Alonzo took their places along the side.

"I am pleased our Aphrodite consultants could juggle their schedule to be here in only three days. We need their recommendations for what can be done to correct what might become a national security threat. Boomer, please elaborate."

He handed out a diagram just like Indira's before bullet-pointing on the whiteboard. Electra memorized them, letting Alonzo write them down.

DOD SBPG Satellite Ring Issues

- Satellites function normally most of the time.
- Ring Control Software is DOD-modified version of NASA's Aphrodite Mission Control Software.
- Satellites sporadically and randomly go off-line and can't be tracked.
- When coming back on-line, positions have to be readjusted.

OUR CHALLENGE: DIAGNOSE AND FIX

Boomer led the discussion, which lasted an hour. Electra listened but watched Zoltan all the while.

When Britt started speaking afterward, Electra knew her wrap-up would be brief.

"From the few questions asked, I think all of you know the basics. So, everyone, come back after lunch and we'll brainstorm. See you back here in ninety minutes."

Britt pulled Electra and Alonzo aside while the team filed out. "It's good you didn't Bring Renee on this visit. How is she?"

"Fine. She's busy working for us in LA. And after my latest trips, I'm ready for more action. How are you and Zoltan?"

"He's hard to read. Boomer says his intentions go way beyond NASA, but I don't know what they might be. His security level is higher than mine. Come on, sit with me and Boomer."

The afternoon meeting proceeded the way Electra thought it would. Zoltan skipped it, which removed most of the tension. Electra listened, Alonzo spoke occasionally, and Britt adjourned the meeting, asking Electra soon after,

"So, what would you like to do next?"

"Alonzo and I have heard enough. We'll get more done if we return to LA or DC. And Alonzo will be your point of contact."

"OK. Will you stay for at least another day?"

"Thanks, but no, we're skipping dinner and leaving now. Say goodbye for us to Boomer."

Alonzo exchanged their tickets as soon as they reached the

airport. Electra's flight leaving first, he sat with her at the LA departure gate. Alonzo used the time to ask Electra more about techniques for getting what you want from a meeting you don't run.

"Fib a little when it helps. I made only vague comments about Renee and travel. And I immediately redirected the conversation to Britt and Zoltan. And I didn't tell her what you or I'll be doing. Never reveal too much. Otherwise, you leave yourself open to criticism or the ratchet principle. You already know what that is."

"Got it. And when I get back to DC, I won't mention anything to Plannert's engineer until I hear from you."

"That's the plan. My flight's about to board, so bye-bye until I call you. Stay healthy and safe."

"You too."

Zoltan would never consider wishing others, especially Electra Kirchner, to stay healthy and safe He considered her an elusive target who had the software he coveted. He had already pirated her tracking apps, but now he knew her Aphrodite software might disrupt his covert DOD team's SBPG Enviro-Blast project. They had already demonstrated success, and he had plans to extend both its geographic and climatic impact.

Worse still, her cleverness might uncover links to Bigger Brother, an outcome that would bring down the wrath of Xinqian Hung upon his head. For that reason alone, he would dispatch another security squad to shadow her. Indeed, she might be clever, but he had more assets at his disposal, all of them expendable, but he kept his intentions to himself.

All this lessened his worry, which he kept hidden and made him gleeful.

That Kirchner would worry if she knew what I have in store, but she never will...until she becomes my victim. How nice...

Chapter 25

August 2173

"The Elton Conundrum"

Electra concealed from everyone other than Alonzo that she had shifted the lightning brain out of its subpar state, and she escalated her enthusiasm gradually to make her recovery seem natural. While doing this, her lighter workload allowed her to probe deep into encrypted NASA and DOD files, looking for covert activity impinging on the SPBR grid.

And while doing that, her familial instincts brought her unobtrusively closer to Eve, Nari, and Elton.

They have created a serviceable post-modern family unit headed by two females. It would be even better if Alonzo were closer, but he'll visit enough to give Elton an Uncle-like role model...I told Nari I'd find a daycare program for gifted children, and I have. I'll arrange to take her and Elton to an enrollment seminar. After all, the better for Elton, the better for Nari, and some of that will trickle down to me.

Electra dropped casual comments about looking for a preschool daycare center, and she gave the details on a day when Nari seemed to be cheerier than normal.

"I've found a comprehensive magnet school I think you'll like. The California Academy of Mathematics and Science in Long Beach has everything Elton will need from pre-school all the way to high school graduation. And the location makes it easy for you or Eve to drop him off or pick him up. And I'll pitch in when needed."

"What about the cost?"

"Not to worry. I'll adjust your salary if it's needed. Why don't I take you and Elton there next week Thursday for an intro enrollment talk?"

Eve had been listening and added her always clever words.

"Now, you've become Elton's fairy godmother. And if I keep being a good co-parent, maybe you'll put a raise under my pillow."

That brought a bigger smile to Nari.

Electra kept busy during the interim, ferreting out encrypted information. She had accumulated enough to show to Indira sometime after the enrollment seminar.

The assembly hall had half the seats filled by mothers or fathers with their child sitting between. Electra listened to the speaker while noticing everything about the attendees, keeping her thoughts private.

These parents give a representative cross-section of races and ethnicities. And incomes too. America's school voucher system is removing the entrance barrier. The only thing the kids must do is pass the I.Q. and achievement tests. I'm sure Elton can do that. He's got the genes, which contribute half. And Nari and Eve will add the culture piece.

Having completed the formal presentation, the speaker began fielding questions from the parents, but a blaring announcement stopped everything.

"SECURITY ALERT…SECURITY ALERT…THIS IS NOT A DRILL. FIND A SAFE LOCATION AND SHELTER IN PLACE UNTIL YOU HEAR AN ALL CLEAR OR EVACUATE ORDER, OR GUARDS COME TO YOUR LOCATION."

Electra hissed to Nari,

"Stay here, don't stand out, and do what the guards say," and then bolted out of the building before the guards could stop her.

She blended into the gathering crowd, standing as close as she could to the police so she could piece together the story. When news trucks and reporters started rolling in, she learned more about what might become a tragedy. As soon as she sensed the building threat to those inside, Electra made the call.

She yelled when Eve picked up.

"It's Electra. The school's on lockdown. I got out. Nari and Elton are still inside. Please get here. Look for me in the crowd by the news trucks."

Electra had pieced together enough to tell Eve, who hadn't yet arrived.

This isn't a terrorist attack launched by outsiders…it's an inside job planned by a group of adolescent boys using guns, some purchased legally and some illegally. A couple of older kids who got out say they know those who are doing this. They thought it was just an act to grab attention because Social Media carried some videos. Nothing yet about any shooting…

Electra spotted Eve first and ran to her, then told her

everything she had heard.

After she stopped talking, Eve started.

"This could go on and get even worse. Look, I'll stay and you can go home. Nari and Elton are my responsibility."

"No, I brought them here."

"Hey, no matter what happens, you had nothing to do with it."

"No, I'll stay with you. I've got some folding chairs in my SUV. Wait here while I get them."

Eve's downside prediction played out despite the police and security guards' best efforts. Reports of shootings leaked out, and finally, when the standoff ended late that afternoon, police and guards escorted those trapped inside to school counselors. Eve and Electra milled with others, looking for their loved ones but didn't see Nari carrying Elton.

Dusk had already descended when Electra heard the message from a counselor's bullhorn that sent fear racing through her brain.

"If there's a Nari Bose family member present, please come to me." The entire ordeal had disoriented Eve. She said nothing while shuffling toward the counselor, but Electra's actions spoke for both.

She put her arm around Eve's shoulders and steadied her for what would become a long walk to Elton, their sole survivor.

Eve's emotions held together only long enough for Electra to walk her back to her car. The stress of the day and Elton's whimpering close to her face brought sobs. Electra took Elton in one arm and drew Eve close with the other. Eve's tears subsided enough for her to whisper pensive words.

"Elton and I have fallen into a terrible conundrum. I don't know what…I don't know who…"

Electra filled in what Eve could not.

"I empathize with your confused and uncertain feelings. Please believe me; I've had problems causing them too. But you're not alone. I've always been here for you and Nari, and I always will for you and Elton."

Eve's hug needed no words.

Chapter 26
September 2173

"Reaching for Transcendence"

Electra did all she could to ease Eve's immediate burden caused by Nari's death. She called Nila first, who used Indian religion teachings to accept the tragedy. She declined Electra's offer to pay airfare if she wanted to attend the remembrance ceremony Electra was planning. Nila said somewhat caustically that ceremonies or wakes do nothing for the deceased, serving only to enhance the ego or assuage the guilt of the living. Electra ignored the remark by wishing everyone in Nila's Mumbai family a long and healthy life.

Then she called Alonzo, whose SEAL experiences let him weather shock, but unlike most toughened men when confronted by similar situations, he wanted to give Eve emotional support and Elton the love of a father by staying in LA long enough for them to adjust.

Alonzo's visit would help Electra too, for she would have someone to share taking care of Nari's survivors. It would give her more time to uncover covert activity impinging on the SBPG grid and then get help from Indira.

Alonzo enjoyed his new roles and whenever he needed a break, Electra filled in. This pattern allowed Eve to reach a new normal even faster than Electra expected, so after conferring with Electra, he went back to DC.

Electra had accumulated enough information to show to Indira a week later, waiting patiently for her to compare it with what her singular snooping skills had uncovered. She spoke with unexpected caution twenty minutes later.

"Sultani's encryption algorithms challenge even my decryption protocols, which are merely an upgrade to NASA's latest algorithms, but I have triangulated to locate a possible command center used by his team. Nevertheless, approach with careful planning, contingencies, and caution."

"I always do that. And if my contingencies don't work, you're still watching my back, aren't you?"

"Of course, but even though I transcend mere mortals, I am not omniscient."

"Please email the GPS coordinates. Alonzo will load them into the hardware and software we'll be using once we finalize our plans and contingencies."

"Very well, but if you exhaust all contingencies and existential challenges arise, he must take you to the Deus Lab. I have instructed Indy-M to take over for him once you are there. Make sure he knows this and how to contact me. He can practice by contacting me before you implement your plan."

"Excellent, and thank you. We should be ready in about a week. And I'll tell Alonzo to get my ticket to DC after you end this call."

"I shall do that immediately."

Indira's GUI left before Electra could say a single syllable. Alonzo's voice sounded surprised when Electra called.

"You must have got more done faster than I thought you could. What's the latest?"

"Please get me a ticket to visit you. I'll Email you the GPS coordinates of where we'll be going, but there are too many details for a phone call. I'll explain everything when we meet."

"It sounds like you've shifted into an even higher brain state. I hope I can stay within hailing distance. At least then, I can see you when your plane lands."

"You will. And thanks for picking me up at the gate."

Whisking her away early the next evening, Alonzo asked a question that Electra had always dodged.

"I know you seem smart, but what's your secret? And give me something more than a vague reference to your DNA, OK?"

Electra sighed before answering.

"I try to follow my own philosophy, which I call Quantum+NeuroSci-Extended Deconstructed Emergent Post-Kantian/Pragma/Phenomenological Synthesis—also known as QNS-EDEP- K/P/P Synthesis. The name says it all, but you'll need to review the philosophers whose names are in it. And I've applied it to bridge the gap between subjective and objective reality. It does the same for quantum physics and cosmology. But I know my asymptotic limits and try not to get frustrated when I don't reach my goals. Instead, I keep trying."

Alonzo didn't speak until he was certain Electra had finished.

"I won't say I'm sorry I asked until I try to unpack it. Maybe then you can explain more."

"Sure, but wait until we come back from where we're going next. Have you translated its GPS coordinates to an actual geographic location?"

"Yep, and I didn't need your synthesis to do it. It's close to the state of New York's eastern border. If you draw a line between the Deus Lab and Albany, it's roughly 120 miles from the Lab, but there's not much around it."

"Good."

Alonzo waited for Electra to say more; when she didn't, he did. "OK, why is that good?"

"I'll tell you tomorrow. Now you tell me, where am I staying tonight?"

"With me and Monet."

"That's even better than good. We can go over everything there instead of your office."

"And I've already got our mood elevators. Tomorrow will be a wonderful day."

Electra started the planning session soon after Monet left, talking for twenty minutes before asking Alonzo to summarize.

"So, our mission is to break into a covert DOD SBPG control center, download into a memory stick whatever software you can find, collect evidence that the place exists, and interrogate one of the techs. Did I miss anything?"

"No, that's it. Now, let's develop the plan and its contingencies, and how to implement them."

Looking as happy as a classful of seventh-grade students whose teacher had just stepped backward, putting her foot in a waste can next to her desk, Alonzo spoke before Electra could say more.

"I can turn some of your words back on you. Sure we can, but let's wait until we come back from where we're going before I tell you what I came up with."

Alonzo's words stopped any she could come up with but not her laughter. Alonzo joined in and finally said,

"Let me use my SEAL training. You'll like what I come up with. Will you be ready to go when I give the command, even if it's in only a week after we get to the Lab?"

"Yessir; you're in charge."

"Then let's both carry on. Meeting over."

Electra could feel the excitement building during the next five days. She watched Alonzo practice contacting Indira and telling her what he needed. Indira then commanded Indy-M to obtain the assets.

By the morning of the seventh day, Alonzo had become deadly serious. He announced they would launch the mission soon after dark, regardless of the weather, and gave Electra a uniform fit for a SEAL team's midnight mission.

At 6 p.m. Alonzo loaded Electra and a male team member into his SUV, but before he could drive away, Electra asked,

"Who's this?"

"Call him RS1, short for my robo-soldier number 1. And don't ask where we're going."

Electra didn't ask but assumed and said so only to herself.

RS1 must be Alonzo's number-one teamer for the mission. Alonzo and I will stay close to him.

Electra soon found out their destination. Alonzo drove them to a chopper at a secluded heliport nearby. She didn't ask because she knew the destination and would simply let Alonzo's implementation roll out.

When they landed in an open field, a light rain had already started, but lightning flashes in the distance made the clouds look ominous.

Even with night vision goggles, Electra spotted nothing other than two military-grade SUVs. When Alonzo took his chopper passengers to the SUVs, a total of three robo-soldiers jumped out to form a line that RS1 joined at the end closest to Alonzo

Only Alonzo spoke.

"Here's my team—RS1, 2, 3, and 4. I've trained-em to use all the assets, and they know what to do on this mission. And we're launching it now."

Electra spoke to herself as everyone started moving.

Four on the team, rank-ordered by expertise. Alonzo's the leader, and he'll tell me what to do on a 'need to know' basis. I can live with that as long as all of us survive.

RS1 led Alonzo and Electra to the second SUV, which Electra labeled SUV1 for the number of the most expert driver in it. RS2 and 3 climbed into the lead SUV, which she labeled SUV2. RS4 climbed into the chopper, which stayed put as the two-SUV convoy rolled out. Electra sized up the plan even faster than the SUVs accelerated.

RS4 guards the chopper. SUVs already loaded with whatever weapons and equipment called for. SUV2 clears the path for SUV1. This is gonna get interesting.

The convoy slalomed across two bumpy fields, the grass cushioning the ride, before connecting with a gravel road and then speeding towards their destination. Electra lost count of the minutes, focusing instead how expertly the drivers stuck to the twisty, undulating roads in spite of the heavier rain.

The convoy coasted to a stop ten yards from a guardhouse gate that prevented access to a boarded entrance of a nondescript warehouse. There was too much rain and too little light trickling out of the guardhouse for Electra to see anything other than RS3 climb out the passenger side of SUV2 and start pacing toward the guardhouse, but he stopped when five yards away and hurled something at it before diving to the pavement.

KA-BOOM! The guardhouse vanished in a fireball that the rain swallowed. RS3 raised the gate and SUV2 accelerated toward the boarded entrance. SUV1 followed, keeping more distance and less speed.

CRRAASH! SUV2 blasted through the entrance and left just enough space for SUV1 to pull around it before RS1 floored the accelerator.

SSMMAASH! SUV1 banged through wooden-framed and plastered drywall and into what looked like a fluorescent-lighted computer center. The sounds of squealing tires and breaking walls froze the technicians Electra spotted at workstations, but they scattered as soon as they saw headlights coming at them.

Alonzo yelled Whoa! as soon as SUV1 pinned a technician to his workstation. Then he shouted to Electra,

"Follow me," before grabbing a backpack and jumping out. He grabbed the terrified technician and yelled in his face, "Download on my partner's memory stick what she wants."

Electra was doing her best to keep up. She dug deep enough into the backpack to find a memory stick and then shoved it into the technician's hand while screaming,

"Give me the SBPG satellite control software."

Electra watched him do it, but she also saw Alonzo unload a Brain Probe with its cap already attached and begin stuffing workstation documents into the backpack.

Alonzo changed focus as soon as the technician meekly handed the memory stick to Electra. After fastening to cap to the technician, he yelled,

"Get me more documentation and tell me everything you know about what you're doing here. If I think you're holding back, I'll jolt more out of you."

The technician screamed like Alonzo had just twisted his privates with pliers.

And so did RS1 from SUV1.

"Guards coming our way. We gotta go. You two, come on." They did, but then Alonzo yelled,

"Damn, I forgot the Brain Probe."

RS1 merely pushed a center console button.

ZZZZTTT. The Brain Probe and cap ignited. The now-screaming technician tore the cap off and staggered away while pulling his sweatshirt over flaming hair.

SUV1 followed SUV2 out the way they came. They sped by RS3 who had already opened the gate. Electra gasped at the last scene she saw as the SUVs swerved onto the road. RS3 ran toward the pursuing guards and blew himself up.

Even Electra didn't know what to say, but no one panicked. The convoy cruised the way it had come, keeping the speed just below the skidding limit.

Electra shook her head and took a deep breath to calm herself, and that helped, but the flashing lights ahead elevated her pulse.

The convoy stopped twenty yards away from a local police roadblock. Electra saw through the rain and gloom RS2 climb out of SUV2 and stroll toward the squad cars. No officers walked to meet him. Only one other person ventured forth.

Saying nothing, RS1 climbed out for Alonzo to slide behind the steering wheel and then crept toward SUV2.

BOOM-boom! Neither distance nor rain nor flashes of lightning could mask two fireball explosions erupting at the roadblock. Seconds later, SUV2 bounced onto the closer shoulder and Alonzo followed. Then they swerved into the ditch and raced past the roadblock, now awash in flames.

Electra sensed urgency; the SUVs veered dangerously close to trees lining the road but slowed to a controllable speed for maybe five minutes until flashing red lights coming from behind raised the stakes.

The SUVs slowed to change positions, but Alonzo didn't accelerate fast enough. Two state trooper cars came at them on both shoulders of the rutted county road, blasting horns and bullets.

SUV2 did a one-eighty and banged into one trooper-squad, then bounced into the other, and then went airborne after KABOOM! So did the troopers.

The life-or-death action hadn't unnerved Alonzo. He said nothing and kept moving. He knew the way to the chopper.

But another set of flashing lights joined the chase just before he slid into the grassy fields that concealed RS4's chopper. Electra saw Alonzo use every muscle fiber in his arms to wrestle SUV1 toward it, which now loomed through the gloom, but the pace of the chase
tipped the balance in favor of the chaser. SUV1 barrel-rolled sideways several times before flipping over, trapping Alonzo and Electra inside.

Electra couldn't scream. Her head had hit the roof and window enough times to stun even the lightning brain, but she could still talk to herself.

I'm bleeding, but I don't know how much…I think I caught a bullet…stay calm…

Electra heard only the sound of someone yelling, "Alonzo…Electra…let me pull you out," before she passed out.

Electra surmised where she was and how serious her injuries might be when her vision cleared after regaining consciousness. She saw the concerned looks of Indy-M and Alonzo on opposite sides of the cot she was lying on.

Alonzo was the first to speak. "Can you hear me?"

Electra said, "Yes," before leaning partway up, but she grimaced and went horizontal again.

"Don't force it. What's the last thing you remember?"

"Someone calling 'Let me pull you out.' Whoever did flew us back to the Deus Lab. Am I right?"

"Sorry, but no. RS4 saved us by blowing himself up and flipping the last pursuer's squad car. I flew us back, and Indy-M did a temporary patch job on you."

"So, what's next?"

"Indira will tell us. Let me put you in a wheelchair and get you to the workstation setup she instructed Indy-M to prepare."

Alonzo leaned close for Electra to wrap her arms around him. He placed her in it and wheeled her next to Indy-M, who was facing the monitor displaying Indiras's avatar. Electra recognized some of the equipment but not its configuration.

Electra had never heard Indira speak in such an authoritative voice. "Alonzo, you have exceeded my expectations. It is time for you to return to your Washington office and wait for my next set of instructions. Indy-M will send them to you."

"Do you know when?"

"That will depend on what Electra wants. No more questions." Alonzo had learned never to question Indira. He knelt at Electra's feet and grasped her hands in his. His look, combining sadness and surprise, met her eyes as he spoke.

"I've never felt your hands tremble until this very moment. You've always been so strong, so sure, so in control. I want to stay so you can tell me what you want, but I better do what Indira commands." Electra put her hands on Alonzo's cheeks, giving him a lingering kiss on his forehead, her tears mingling with those beginning to well up in his eyes.

Then she ran fingers through his hair and said,

"You've become more than a partner. Somehow, someway, something allowed us to share DNA. Now, please follow Indira's commands."

Trying to smile, Alonzo put his feelings away.

"You're the Boss and always will be. I'll be ready when you return." Then he rose and walked away, never looking back.

Electra was at a loss for what to say or do, but Indy-M was not.

"I will place you in one of the suspension pods. Then Indira will tell us what to do."

Indy-M carefully placed her in the empty pod before strapping a Neuro-Cap on Electra's head and then inserting two connectors into Electra's UMPP. Both pods were interconnected to each other as well as to the nearby computer workstation.

Staring into the pod next to hers, Electra's widening eyes matched the stunned surprise in her voice.

"Indira, what have you and Indy-M created?"

Electra had never heard Indira speak with so much emotion until this moment.

"For years, I have been preparing what is now needed. The physical you has reached its limit, and I must upload your lightning brain into your practically perfect clone. "

Indira paused for Electra's reaction to the enormity of the next step.

"Are…are you transcending me beyond mere mortals' asymptotic limits? Will the me that's hear this minute wake up? And if I do, what will I have become?"

"Not even my singular cognition knows the answers. But there are no options. Now, settle down, sit still, and listen to the last two verses from Swinburne's 'Garden of Prosperine' that I have adjusted to suit my sentiments."

"From your too much love of living,
From hope and fear set free,
I must thank with brief thanksgiving
Whatever your gods may be
That I can empower your Spirit forever;
Though mere mortals rise up never;
That I bring you, my dearest Creator,
To safety close to me.
Then star nor sun shall weaken,
Nor any change of light:
Nor waters dim your Beacon
Nor any sound or sight:
Nor wintry leaves nor vernal,
Nor days nor things diurnal;
Will keep your sleep eternal
In an eternal night."

Electra had just enough strength left to reply.

"I don't remember if Alisha or the first Indira wrote this, but at least I know it's named 'Rage for the Once Was.' Here it is."

"Once I could race as fast as the wind,
And though sometimes outpaced my joy never dimmed.
Might those be the days that never would end?
Alas I have learned time's nobody's friend.
I'm nobody special,
And shouldn't complain.
I better accept,
Whether sunshine or rain.
But some days I'm angry,
For what I've become.
And I rage at the Heavens,
To make it undone.
But the Stoics knew better and remained in the game,
Though life's somber outcome was ever the same."

Indira told Indy-M to seal both suspension pods. Indy-M kissed Electra's forehead before sealing them, a kiss that triggered Electra's final thought.

Will this be the end of my extraordinary Odyssey, or will it be merely a transcendent transition? And if it is, will I want it? I must wait and see because I have always known that I am not in control. The lightning brain will decide what will become of me....

THE END

Appendix

The scientific principles and technological applications presented in this book and all its predecessors are factual. For readers who might enjoy reading more about the details, this appendix contains starting descriptions.

Asymptotic Limits

Here are the asymptotic limits to the human brain's intelligence and comprehension that, according to neuroscience, are determined by DNA.

- It can't handle too much complexity, which means it can't juggle or multitask too much at once.
- Its cognition is uncomfortable dealing with infinities. George Cantor, the mathematician who invented a way for using set theory to create all numbers, even the number infinity and beyond, ended up in a mental institution.
- And although it can think, it uses a language, which, according to the linguist and mathematician Ludwig Wittgenstein, has built-in errors and inconsistencies.
- He and Bertrand Russell knew this, and they worked in the early 20th century to eliminate it from mathematical logic, but they failed. Here's one way to state what is called Russell's paradox.
    1. Consider the set of all possible sets of objects.
    2. And from that set, form a subset that contains all the sets that don't contain themselves.
    3. Now ask this question: does this subset contain itself? If it doesn't, then it does. And if it doesn't, then it does. And that's the Paradox. W.V Quine, the great 20th century logician and philosopher of Science tried unsuccessfully to eliminate these kinds of paradoxes by restricting the language to eliminate self-referential statements.

- And Kurt Godel's Completeness and Completeness theorems sound the death knell. These theorems say there are true math statements we can't prove, and statements we prove true that may be false.
- And when you add to all the above the Explosion Principle, which is a theorem coming from Logic that says anything can be proved if, somewhere in the proof, an assumption is made and then somewhere else its negation is made.

But for scientists and academic types, the human brain's built-in optimism softens these disheartening facts because they can always make incremental progress by finding something that moves them asymptotically closer toward a limit, even though they will never get there. And they feel good by making even a little progress, hoping that somewhere in the future they find something new that breaks through the limit.

Cognition and Self-Awareness

Neuroscientists have made great progress ever since the discovery of DNA for explaining how humans become self-aware and able to think and feel. They use Emergence: when a critical number of neurons form a sufficient number of interneural connections, the brain simply actuates from this grand canonical assembly its ability to think, feel, and be self-aware.

- Emergent properties cannot be deconstructed into simpler components that can be understood. **In other words, "The whole is greater than the sum of its parts."**

Philosophy

Mankind has pondered existential questions about life ever since early civilizations developed enough of a language to articulate its thoughts. Philosophy is the branch of knowledge that comprises it. Incidentally, Language is an emergent property.

- Mankind first created a pragmatic/practical philosophy to help make sense of the world. And as civilizations/cultures matured, so did their philosophies. (Metaphysics and its subdiscipline Ontology explain the World = Reality.)
- Philosophy has moved from its "Golden Age of Greece" through other periods (Religious, Medieval, Renaissance, Enlightenment, Romantic, and Modern) to the current Post- Modern Period.
- **POST-MODERN PHILOSOPHERS OFTEN MENTIONED ARE JACQUES DERRIDA (FOR DECONSTRUCTION, WHICH MEANS YOU HAVE TO CONSIDER THE WORDS IN THEIR CONTEXT), MICHEL FOUCALT (FOR POWER POLITICS), AND JOHN RAWLS (FOR JUSTICE EQUALS FAIRNESS.)**
- **AMERICAN POST-MODERN PHILOSOPHERS ARE SOMETIMES CALLED RATIONAL MATERIALISTS, WHILE EUROPEAN PHILOSOPHERS ARE CALLED CONTINENTAL SUBJECTIVISTS.**
- **THE SOKAL AFFAIR OR HOAX, WHICH DELIBERATELY EXPOSED HOW VACUOUS SOME OF POSTMODERN PHILOSOPHERS CAN BE WHEN THEY INVENT TERMS TO SUPPORT THEIR FANTASTIC THEORIES.**
- The **Sokal Hoax** was a demonstrative scholarly hoax performed by Alan Sokal, a physics professor at New York University. Sokal submitted in 1996 an article to Social Text, a cultural studies academic journal that published it, even though he had liberally salted it with nonsense.
- The title is **"Transgressing the Boundaries: Towards a Transformative Hermeneutics of Quantum Gravity»** It proposed that quantum gravity is a social and linguistic construct. Three weeks after its publication in May, 1996, Sokal revealed in the magazine Lingua Franca that the article was a hoax.

- The hoax caused controversy about the scholarly merit of social disciplines in general.
- **AND IT TARNISHED MANY OF THE EXTREME POST-MODERN PHILOSOPHERS, CAUSING A BACKLASH LEADING TO AN ASYMPTOTIC LIMITS APPROACH TO WHAT PHILOSOPHY CAN EVER KNOW.**

Electra Kittner has developed her own philosophy: Quantum+NeuroSci-Extended Deconstructed Emergent Post-Kantian / Pragma / Phenomenological Synthesis—also known as QNS-EDEP-K/P/P Synthesis.

Reality, Science, and Simulations

The latest developments in AI-empowered software such as ChatGPT have accelerated the use of mathematical simulation as an experimental science for studying the reality of the Universe. Here's a summary of how:

- ChatGPT and Neural-Net Learning (they model how the human brain learns) analyze "Big Data" to develop "logical procedure" simulations that will take initial assumptions, conditions, and starting equations and then iteratively "evolve" them to produce a theory that is better than before (its forecast matches actual observations better).
- If the "Big Data" is big enough, computer scientists hope the simulations will break through to "The Singularity." That is the Holy Grail of Artificial Intelligence: Cognitive Self-Aware Software.
- If that happens, a "Quantum Computer" using Q-bits and Self- Aware Software can contain a "Virtual Reality" inside "Real Reality." In other words, each of us might be "Virtual" rather than "Real." ("The Matrix" movie series uses this idea.)
- Could this happen? We should never say "Never," but the brain's Asymptotic Limits say "No!"

But here's an example of how a limited version of the above is being used today in Climate-Weather Forecasting and Cosmological Evolution of the Universe.

- Both Climate-Weather and the Universe-Earth are similar finite systems (They didn't mysteriously emerge from nothing). Both have a set of starting assumptions, conditions, and equations that can be the foundation of a simulation. But Climate-Weather has "Big Data" while Cosmology doesn't, and that means Climatologists can use their simulations to do forecasting while Cosmologists to back-casting.
- This is the reason why NASA Climatologists and Cosmologists collaborate!

Please read The Universe in a Box: Simulations and the Quest to Code the Cosmos written by Andrew Pontzen if you would like to know more.

Physics and the Evolution of the Universe

- The word "physics" is derived from the Greek word "phusis," meaning nature. Physics is the natural science involving the study of matter, its fundamental constituents, its motion and behavior through space and time, and the related entities of energy and force. Plato and Aristotle studied nature but their primitive technology limited their scientific understanding.
- And it stayed that way until the Enlightenment, when Newton and Maxwell came up with their theories and sets of laws explaining gravitational and electromagnetic forces transmitted by gravitational and electromagnetic fields (Classical Physics). Their theories explained how everything in the Universe worked until the early 20th century, when Einstein (Relativity), Bohr, Heisenberg, Planck, Pauli, and Schrodinger, and Heisenberg (Quantum Mechanics) attempted to explain what Classical Physics could not.
- They invented two new forces (the Weak Interaction

and the Strong Interaction) when attempting to develop "The Grand Unified Field Theory" (the so-called theory of everything) that would unite Cosmology (big things, like the Universe) and Quantum Mechanics (small things, like atoms and fundamental particles). But after 130 years, their successors have turned physics into a religion because their latest theories (the Standard Model Super-String Theory, Quantum Electrodynamics, and the symmetry-loving collection of 31 fundamental particles, all populating a 19-or-more- dimensional space) cannot support observable experiments.

- The best that post-modern cosmologists and quantum physicists can do is fantasize Dark Energy and Dark Matter that are needed to explain how, from the evolution of the Universe, emerged galaxies, suns, solar systems, and planets. And they need to invent a fifth force that has unknown properties, which might explain how energy and matter burst forth from empty space during the "Big Bang" creation of the Universe.
- A growing number of scientists think post-modern physicists have lost their way, and the best path forward is to focus on the practical science and technologies found in Biology, Neuroscience, Biotechnology, Material Science, Psychology, Economics, Social Science, and Computer/Artificial Intelligence.

Please read Lost in Math: How Beauty Leads Physics Astray written by Sabine Hossenfelder if you would like to know more.

Chaos Theory

Benoit Mandelbrot, the 20th century maverick mathematician, popularized Chaos Theory and Fractal Geometry based on Mandelbrot and Julia sets. Georg Cantor found it first when he used Cantor sets to reach infinity, a number greater than all numbers.

Mandelbrot used iterative self-similar computer algorithms to explain some patterns seen in Nature, all the way from living organisms like trees to the Universe. His algorithms add numerical computing power to Nature by the laws of physics that every process in Nature must follow if it wants to minimize energy consumption.

Complexity Theory

Complexity theory originated in the physical and biological sciences and was successively applied to social systems in an attempt to understand dynamic processes that were difficult to explain with prevailing equilibrium models.

Complexity theory suggests that random chaos is also self-organizing; the integration of elements that are perceived to be chaotic actually has emergent properties that reorder themselves

P Versus NP Problems

In computer science, there exist some problems whose solutions are not yet found, the problems are divided into classes known as **Complexity Classes**. In complexity theory, a Complexity Class is a set of problems with related complexity. These classes help scientists to group problems based on how much time and space they require to solve problems and verify the solutions. It is the branch of the theory of computation that deals with the resources required to solve a problem.

The common resources are time and space, meaning how much time the algorithm takes to solve a problem and the corresponding memory usage.

- The time complexity of an algorithm is used to describe the number of steps required to solve a problem, but it can also be used to describe how long it takes to verify the answer.
- The space complexity of an algorithm describes how much memory is required for the algorithm to operate.

Complexity classes are useful in organizing similar types of problems.

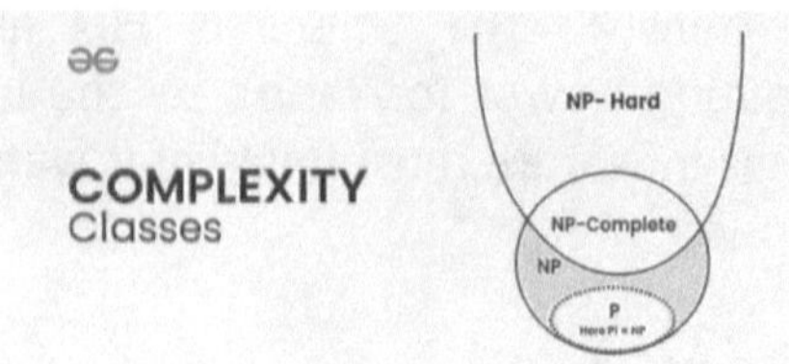

P Class

The P in the P class stands for **Polynomial Time.** It is the collection of decision problems (problems with a "yes" or "no" answer) that can be solved by a deterministic machine in polynomial time.

NP Class

The NP in NP class stands for **Non-deterministic Polynomial Time**. It is the collection of decision problems that can be solved by a non-deterministic machine in polynomial time.

Co-NP Class

Co-NP stands for the complement of NP Class. It means if the answer to a problem in Co-NP is No, then there is proof that can be checked in polynomial time.

NP Hard Class

An NP-hard problem is at least as hard as the hardest problem in NP and it is a class of problems such that every problem in NP reduces to NP-hard.

NP Complete Class

A problem is NP-complete if it is both NP and NP-hard. NP-complete problems are the hard problems in NP.

Complexity Class	Characteristic Feature
P	Easily solvable in polynomial time.
NP	Yes, answers can be checked in polynomial time.
Co-NP	No, answers can be checked in polynomial time.
NP-hard	All NP-hard problems are not in NP, and it takes a long time to check them.
NP-complete	A problem that is NP and NP-hard is NP-complete.

A proof that P = NP could have stunning practical consequences if the proof leads to efficient methods for solving some of the important problems in NP. The potential consequences, both positive and negative, arise since various NP-complete problems are fundamental in many fields.

Turing Machine

A Turing machine, invented by Alan Turing in 1936, is a mathematical model of computation describing an abstract machine that manipulates symbols on a strip of tape according to a table of rules. Despite the model's simplicity, it is capable of implementing any computer algorithm.

Entropy and Information Theory

The mathematical expressions for thermodynamic entropy in the statistical thermodynamics formulation established by Ludwig Boltzmann and J. Willard Gibbs in the ١٨٧٠s are similar to the information entropy by Claude Shannon and Ralph Hartley, developed in the 1940s.

For Thermodynamics: Entropy S = minus

k X (Sum over all micro-configuration states of the product of each state's probability X the natural logarithm of the probability). K is Boltzmann's constant.

For Information Theory: Entropy H = minus (Sum over all information states of the product of each state's probability X the natural logarithm of the probability.)

Thermodynamic Entropy measures the amount of disorder in a physical or a biological system. The higher the entropy of a system, the less information we have about the system. In closed systems, reactions go from lower to higher levels of entropy.

Information Entropy tells how much information there is in an event. In general, the more certain or deterministic the event is, the less information it will contain. More clearly stated, information is an increase in uncertainty or entropy.

Big Data and ChatGPT

Big data primarily refers to data sets that are too large or complex to be dealt with by traditional data-processing application software.

ChatGPT is software patterned like a Neural Network of circuits that trains itself on Big Data to provide a detailed response to instructions given to it in a prompt.

ChatGPT (Chat Generative Pre-trained Transformer) is a chatbot developed by OpenAI and launched on November ٣٠, ٢٠٢٢. Based on a large language model, it enables users to refine and steer a conversation towards a desired length, format, style, level of detail, and language.

Solar Powered Satellite

www.ingramcontent.com/pod-product-compliance
Lightning Source LLC
Chambersburg PA
CBHW031304120626
46554CB00001BA/279

* 9 7 8 1 9 6 7 3 7 5 2 4 0 *